T0214621

IFIP Advances in Information and Communication Technology

571

Editor-in-Chief

Kai Rannenberg, Goethe University Frankfurt, Germany

Editorial Board Members

IFIP – The International Federation for Information Processing

IFIP was founded in 1960 under the auspices of UNESCO, following the first World Computer Congress held in Paris the previous year. A federation for societies working in information processing, IFIP's aim is two-fold: to support information processing in the countries of its members and to encourage technology transfer to developing nations. As its mission statement clearly states:

> IFIP is the global non-profit federation of societies of ICT professionals that aims at achieving a worldwide professional and socially responsible development and application of information and communication technologies.

IFIP is a non-profit-making organization, run almost solely by 2500 volunteers. It operates through a number of technical committees and working groups, which organize events and publications. IFIP's events range from large international open conferences to working conferences and local seminars.

The flagship event is the IFIP World Computer Congress, at which both invited and contributed papers are presented. Contributed papers are rigorously refereed and the rejection rate is high.

As with the Congress, participation in the open conferences is open to all and papers may be invited or submitted. Again, submitted papers are stringently refereed.

The working conferences are structured differently. They are usually run by a working group and attendance is generally smaller and occasionally by invitation only. Their purpose is to create an atmosphere conducive to innovation and development. Refereeing is also rigorous and papers are subjected to extensive group discussion.

Publications arising from IFIP events vary. The papers presented at the IFIP World Computer Congress and at open conferences are published as conference proceedings, while the results of the working conferences are often published as collections of selected and edited papers.

IFIP distinguishes three types of institutional membership: Country Representative Members, Members at Large, and Associate Members. The type of organization that can apply for membership is a wide variety and includes national or international societies of individual computer scientists/ICT professionals, associations or federations of such societies, government institutions/government related organizations, national or international research institutes or consortia, universities, academies of sciences, companies, national or international associations or federations of companies.

More information about this series at http://www.springer.com/series/6102

Eunika Mercier-Laurent · Danielle Boulanger (Eds.)

Artificial Intelligence for Knowledge Management

5th IFIP WG 12.6 International Workshop, AI4KM 2017
Held at IJCAI 2017
Melbourne, VIC, Australia, August 20, 2017
Revised Selected Papers

 Springer

Editors
Eunika Mercier-Laurent (iD)
University of Reims Champagne-Ardenne
Reims, France

Danielle Boulanger
Jean Moulin University Lyon 3
Lyon, France

ISSN 1868-4238   ISSN 1868-422X (electronic)
IFIP Advances in Information and Communication Technology
ISBN 978-3-030-29906-4   ISBN 978-3-030-29904-0 (eBook)
https://doi.org/10.1007/978-3-030-29904-0

This Springer imprint is published by the registered company Springer Nature Switzerland AG
The registered company address is: Gewerbestrasse 11, 6330 Cham, Switzerland

Preface

IJCAI 2017 https://www.ijcai.org/proceedings/2017/ was more diversified than the previous, covering all fields of AI. We did not find "Knowledge Management," but main components were considered, such as: knowledge representation, dynamics of knowledge, knowledge base, knowledge transfer, shared knowledge, knowledge engineering, visual knowledge, and combining knowledge with deep convolutional neural networks.

Understanding the benefits of Knowledge Management for research, organizations and businesses and application is still a challenge for many. The overall process involving people, big data, and all kinds of computers and applications has a potential of acceleration discovery and innovation from organized and optimized flow of knowledge. This book's aim is to challenge researchers and practitioners to better explore all of AI fields and integrate world feedback from experience.

Knowledge Management is a large multidisciplinary field rooted in Management and Artificial Intelligence. AI brought forth the way of thinking, knowledge modeling, knowledge processing, and problem solving techniques. Knowledge is one of the intangible capitals that influence the performance of organizations and their capacity to innovate. Since the beginning of the KM movement in the early nineties, companies and nonprofit organizations have experimented with various approaches.

After the first AI4KM (Artificial Intelligence for Knowledge Management) organized by IFIP (International Federation for Information Processing) group TC12.6 (Knowledge Management) in partnership with the European Conference on Artificial Intelligence (ECAI 2012), and the second workshop held during the Federated Conferences on Computer Science and Information Systems (Fedcsis 2014) in conjunction with the Knowledge Acquisition and Management conference (KAM). The third manifestation has begun a partnership with the International Joint Conference on Artificial Intelligence (IJCAI) since 2015. The fourth AI4KM was held during IJCAI 16, New York and the fifth in Melbourne, Australia, co-located with IJCAI 17.

The objective of this multidisciplinary conjunction is still to raise the interests of AI researchers and practitioners in Knowledge Management challenges, to discuss methodological, technical, and organizational aspects of AI used for Knowledge Management, and to share the feedback on KM applications using AI.

We would like to thank the members of the Program Committee, who reviewed the papers and helped put together an interesting program in Melbourne. We would also like to thank all authors and our invited talks Dr. Dickson Lukose, Artificial Intelligence Scientist and Data Scientist, GCs Agile, and Bao QuocVo from the School of Software and Electrical Engineering, Faculty of Science, Engineering and Technology, Swinburne University of Technology. Finally, our thanks go out to the local Organizing Committee and all the supporting institutions and organizations.

This volume contains selected papers presented during the workshop. After the presentation, the authors were asked to extend their proposals by highlighting their original thoughts. The selection focused on new contributions in any research area concerning the use of all AI fields for Knowledge Management. An extended Program Committee then evaluated the last versions of the proposals, leading to these proceedings.

The first article is devoted to Knowledge Management in corporations based on synergy between people and technology. The author points out the barriers and benefits of such an approach.

This is followed by an overview of IT tools for management of Knowledge Processes; the authors discuss their efficiency.

The next article titled "Selected Knowledge Management Aspects in Modern Education," put emphasis on learning organization. The long-life learning should be based on Knowledge Management principles and combine various methods available.

The management of IT projects is more efficient and smarter with Knowledge Management, allowing the reuse and optimizing tasks with AI techniques.

The authors of "Dynamics Aspects of Knowledge Evolution," propose introducing a knowledge adoption process and an ontology-aided encapsulation knowledge model to track the changes in Knowledge Bases.

This article is then followed by those describing efforts in preservation of craftsmen know-how in Morocco through four stages of knowledge modeling for future uses.

With the rising concern surrounding planet protection, eco-design is now practiced in companies. Aiming to share eco-design practice, this article proposes modeling the related knowledge and experience.

The next article concerns the influence of stress on crisis management. Authors define a model to predict and measure the impact of stress on actors in a given situation on collaborative crisis management.

The authors of "Detecting Influential Users in Social Networks: Analysing Graph-Based and Linguistic Perspectives," deal with a very hot topic of influence and especially bad influence via social networks using natural language processing.

The last article is related to the previous as it addresses the problem of global security and focuses on video analysis with the aim of preventing terrorist actions.

The above papers cover machine learning, knowledge models, KM and Web, Knowledge capturing and learning, and KM and AI intersection.

We hope that you will enjoy reading these papers.

May 2019

Eunika Mercier-Laurent
Danielle Boulanger
Mieczyslaw Owoc

Organization

Co-editors

Eunika Mercier-Laurent	University of Reims Champagne Ardenne, France
Danielle Boulanger	Jean Moulin University Lyon 3, France

Program Committee

Danielle Boulanger	Jean Moulin University Lyon 3, France
Anne Dourgnon	EDF, France
Otthein Herzog	Jacobs University, Germany
Knut Hinkelmann	University of Applied Sciences and Arts, Switzerland
Gülgün Kayakutlu	Istanbul Technical University, Turkey
Antoni Ligęza	AGH University of Science and Technology, Poland
Helena Lindskog	Linköping University, Sweden
Nada Matta	Troyes Technical University, France
Eunika Mercier-Laurent	University of Reims Champagne Ardenne, France
Mieczysław Lech Owoc	Wroclaw University of Economics, Poland
Frédérique Segond	Bertin Research, France
Guillermo Simari	Universidad Nacional del Sur in Bahia Blanca, Argentina
Janusz Wojtusiak	George Mason University, USA

Local Organizing Committee

Eunika Mercier-Laurent	University of Reims Champagne Ardenne, France
Andy Song	RMIT University, Australia
Dicson Lukose	GCS Agile, Australia
Abdul Sattar	Griffith University, Australia

Organization

Co-editors

Program Committee

Contents

Knowledge Management in Corporations – Synergy Between People and Technology. Barriers and Benefits of Implementation

Łukasz Przysucha[✉]

Wroclaw University of Economics,
Komandorska 118/120, 53-345 Wroclaw, Poland
lukasz.przysucha@ue.wroc.pl

Abstract. Knowledge management is a strategic process in organizations and companies, which is increasingly recognized by both managers and employees. Modern companies try to maximize their gains in different ways. The increasing competition and more advanced management methods in companies are the reason for exploring new possibilities by managers. This article aims to describe implementation process of knowledge management in business and organizations by using modern technologies and verify barriers, which can stop these processes. The author, on basis of researches, verifies opportunities of optimization factors affecting knowledge management, in order to obtain the highest performance and effectiveness of employees.

The article is divided into four parties: the first part defines process of knowledge management and also knowledge, its types and directions for use. The second section presents barriers in organizations, describes why the knowledge is not use enough and not arrive to circulation of information in companies. The next chapter presents technologies of knowledge management, especially CMS that are not still discovered, but can be the great supports for processes in organizations. In the last part, the author suggests solutions, which can reduce barrier and problems of knowledge management in companies using suitable technologies.

Keywords: Knowledge management · Company · Barriers · Benefits · Content management systems · CMS

1 Introduction

In recent years, many organizations have recognized that the assets are not only important in organization's life. People, human capital, influences decisively on effectiveness and performance of company and decide about final gains. The knowledge management [1] is a compilation containing methods of gathering, managing, capturing and using knowledge, both explicit and tacit [2, 3]. Explicit knowledge [4] is knowledge that can be readily articulated, codified, accessed and verbalized [5]. It is easy to transfer this kind of knowledge to others. Most forms of explicit knowledge can be stored in certain media [6]. There is many examples of explicit knowledge like the data contained in books and encyclopedias. Tacit knowledge is the kind of knowledge

E. Mercier-Laurent and D. Boulanger (Eds.): AI4KM 2017, IFIP AICT 571, pp. 1–11, 2019.
https://doi.org/10.1007/978-3-030-29904-0_1

that is difficult to transfer to another person by means of writing it down or verbalizing it [7, 8]. For example, that Paris is in the France is a part of explicit knowledge that can be written down, transmitted, and understood by a recipient. However, the ability to speak English, walk on the street or play a piano use complex equipment requires all sorts of knowledge that is not always known explicitly, even by expert practitioners, and which is difficult or impossible to explicitly transfer to other people. Knowledge management is, in part, an attempt of the best possible use of knowledge, which is available in organization, creation of a new knowledge and growth of knowledge understands [9, 10]. There are many types of knowledge management. The author suggests the easiest distribution of the activities, which are necessary in the human resources management [11–13] (Fig. 1).

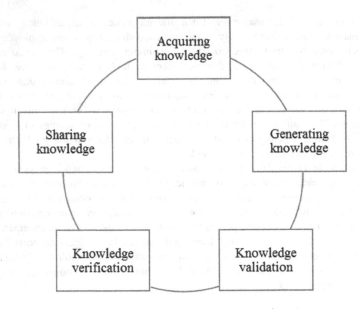

Fig. 1. Scheme of knowledge management cycle processes

The first phase focuses on acquiring knowledge from the environment. At this stage, the information come from outside of the organization. The employees, who have knowledge of specific subjects, verify which areas will be used in the further process. It is also important to show a role of metadata, which determinate methods of acquiring knowledge and present the best practice. This phase defines the goals and steps for managing the special areas and attributes and recipient are allocated. The next phase is generating knowledge. The tools, which support knowledge management and learning, are useful here. The author believes that content management system, which is described later in the next chapter, by standardizing and creating parts in common with KM can be massive support for knowledge management processes in company. Nowadays, the knowledge is aggregated in systems and there is no place for rating, only collecting and fixing. It should be remembered about secure access to confidential information. Gaining knowledge from the organization can support market competition and even eliminate our company.

The next step is valuing knowledge, sorting it, prioritizing and eliminating unnecessary content. Dedicated staff rates aggregation of content by degree of importance and next the knowledge is disseminated. The knowledge gained from employees and external processes, segregated and valued according to previously determined criteria is available for organizational units in accordance with thematic scope and demand for it. The intellectual capital is growing, the employees are learning, exchanging the information and using procedures, which improve these processes. The last stage is about exploiting knowledge, what means that employees use the new knowledge in practice. Thanks of their new skills and experience they can work more effective and create the new areas in the company, which contributes to maximizing the organization's gains. Whole five-processes cycle creates comprehensive tool for the knowledge management in organization.

The knowledge management brings many benefits for the companies. The strategy of implementation the knowledge management programme that is optimized properly can increase the efficiency of employees in the organization. The main advantages of implementation the knowledge management procedures are:

A. *Improve customer service by reduce the response time.*

Thanks to the fact that the knowledge is located in the single place and facilitation of searching the information, it is possible to reduce customer-waiting time for the answers and orders. The company contains the full information to focus on specific topic and the answers are confirmed by the data of the knowledge management process.

B. *Optimization of employee's rotation in the company.*

The process of the knowledge management can be linked with staff hiring and whole Human Resources department. The analysis of aggregation knowledge process can brings managers date about level of knowledge of their employees or even about their investment for company development. Thanks to this fact the managers can identify the most talented and resourceful employees.

C. *More innovation in teams.*

The aggregation and the information management which are received by employees, may be affected more creativity and creates new ideas for organization's development. Different views for many topics and interdisciplinary of many aspects in single place can support innovation and brings the company the new elements of strategy.

D. *Reduction of cost of running business.*

In case of specific knowledge about the markets and the company, attention should be paid to potential action that may reduce costs of system functioning and remove unnecessary processes. The time needed to useless operations may be redirect to other important processes and actions.

E. *A coherent strategy.*

Thanks to the fact that the knowledge is well organized, it is more uncomplicated to create the organization's strategy. The competition analysis and the estimation of other company's actions is easier than ever.

The knowledge management process is beneficial for the company. These, described above, advantages may increase the gains of the organization by providing competitive advantage, optimizing processes in the company and select the appropriate staff in terms of merit, value as well as quantity. It is very hard to look for faults in this process. The only downside may be the accumulation of all knowledge in one place. In case of interception of this data by the competition, the company may go bankrupt. This strategic place can be considered as a core of business. Some data may be useless using third parties because they are not information but only data [3]. Particular attention should be paid to the security of systems that will hold file collections, and to plan the permissions and topology of attributes assigned to individual employees. It is important that the data access hierarchy is maintained. There may be multiple approaches to sharing data, for example, some companies will decide to publicize the full range of knowledge for all employees, regardless of the degree in the company hierarchy. Others, however, can share employees with those who are outsourced, internal to the company, and those still in the ordinary, managers and management. Each of them will have a different scope of information disseminated. Breakdown can also be based on the content of the departments concerned, but this will reduce the interdisciplinary and creativity of the public.

2 Barriers in Organizations

There are many barriers in the literature that exist in the area of knowledge management. Any signal that prevents the transfer of knowledge should be passed to the environment. Often, employees avoid feedback on problems and barriers that block the whole organizational unit/company process. The author tried to find the most common barriers of sharing knowledge in the organization. According to the study, the problems were divided into 3 groups (Fig. 2).

The research indicated that the two most numerous groups of problems are individual and organizational. Below are potential individual barriers to sharing knowledge in organizations:

A. *No time to share knowledge.*

Due to the distribution of work in organizational units, it is not possible to talk with other employees and exchange experiences and perceptions of the problems.

B. *Varied level of knowledge and experience.*

Due to the different levels of proficiency in the company, employees have barriers in conversation such as junior-senior.

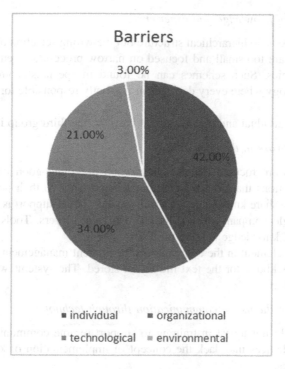

Fig. 2. Barriers related to the exchange of knowledge in an enterprise

C. *Low awareness of the owned knowledge and benefits flowing from it.*

Employees are often unaware of the fact that they are rich in knowledge and can expand it by exchanging with others.

D. *Other differences such as age difference or sex.*

Employees avoid direct contact with others due to differences in age, sex, job seniority, the scope of activities performed on a daily basis.

The second area is organizational barriers. These include:

A. *Wrong company management.*

Lack of supervision, weak leadership, managers unaware of the benefits of exchanging knowledge. Company strategy does not capture knowledge management. The goals in the company are unclear and unspecified.

B. *There is no company resources to share.*

It is important that the conditions in the company guarantee the exchange of knowledge. This is not only about hardware and the latest technologies, but also about real places such as shared social rooms.

C. Varied level of knowledge and experience.

At this point, there is no hierarchical structure but the wrong selection of organizational units. Often they are too small and focused on narrow processes so employees cannot analyze other topics. Such schemes can be found in specialist companies such as advanced technology where every department is strictly responsible for a narrow range of work.

Apart from individual and organizational barriers, the third group is technological.

A. No social network in the company.

Many companies are focused on providing employees with good contact with colleagues. Organizations that do not attach much importance to their peer relationships and willingness to share knowledge are much smaller. Great support is social networks running in a single company in the cloud or on local servers. Tools include instant messaging, chats, knowledge sharing portals.

An important element in the company can be content management systems, which will serve as a backbone for the text file layers stored. The systems will be discussed later in this chapter.

B. No training in the use of communication through technology.

Companies that do not invest in training to support remote communications through tele-informatics devices may lack the concept of implementation of knowledge management processes.

These barriers can vary to some extent in reducing the success of implementing a knowledge management process in a company. Establishing a unified, standardized knowledge management system can certainly optimize these processes, encourage employees to engage, and manage data realistically in all organizational units. The author believes that Electronic Content Management Systems, especially those based on GNU GPL such as WordPress, Drupal, Joomla, can largely meet the needs of a content management and knowledge company and their legal personality and license to use free and develop projects lead to competitiveness with paid counterparts dedicated to the target entities.

3   Technologies Supporting Knowledge Management - CMS

One of the most important elements for implementing knowledge management in a company is technology that allows free exchange of information. Many companies focus on advanced systems that will support processes. The author suggests the development and opening of content management systems available under the GNU GPL, which are based on open source. Many platforms like WordPress, Joomla and Drupal are currently only used to publish raw data on the Internet. Some of them have functionality enhanced with community and multimedia features. In this chapter, they will be characterized and described with reference to Knowledge Management implementation.

Content management is the sum of processes [14] and technologies that help manage process, collect and publish information in a variety of forms.

There are several types of content in CMS. The best known is the content displayed on the browser screen. It is primarily text, graphics, graphs, videos, animations, and the interface of the system. In addition, on the server side there are counterparts to the displayed content, their components, generators and content contained in the database. The administrator operates on processes, programs, and algorithms. It also includes metadata such as formats, schemes, objects for content authors, creation dates, expiration, etc.

The entire content management process has many meanings in different perspectives [15]:

A. *From the point of view of business objectives, CM distributes business value.*
B. *From an analytical perspective, it balances organizational forces.*
C. *From a professional point of content management combines the individual in the organization.*
D. *From the perspective of the process, CM collects, manages and publishes information.*
E. *From a technical perspective, content management is a technical infrastructure.*

All systems, regardless of their mode of operation and location of use, have one main objective - the optimal and efficient management of data and information. Each of them has a basic set of features that is also repeated in other software.

A. *Monitoring and control of content - division of roles and the creation of hierarchies with rights for individual users, content security.*
B. *Verification of content in the system and data coming from the outside.*
C. *Managing the entire document cycle - from creation, modification and use, to disposal.*
D. *Search keyword optimization.*
E. *Ability to create reports.*
F. *In some cases the publication of the content.*

Content management systems are dynamic pages. At the outset, it is useful to define the concept of static and dynamic pages, and to define the differences between them.

Classic, static pages flourished in the 90 s of the last century. Currently static standardization has been abandoned and moved to dynamic sites.

Static pages are portals [16] that do not change their content when called in a user's browser. In order to make any changes to the page, the administrator is forced to overwrite the files manually. Simple pages, based on HTML, have both advantages and disadvantages. They are quite easy to prepare and the whole process of creating a website is fast. There are freeware wizards on the market that allow you to modify portals without the knowledge of the language. Preparing a static website does not require a lot of effort, so it is cheap. The greatest use of such sites is for simple www business cards. They do not require a server with PHP support and MySQL databases. Hosting can also be free. Unfortunately, when user send a page to the server and make modifications to it, basic knowledge of creating websites is essential. The biggest drawback is the lack of interaction with users. These pages only serve to convey unilateral information without any action on the user-administrator line. They are usually less interesting than dynamic and users spend less time on them (Fig. 3).

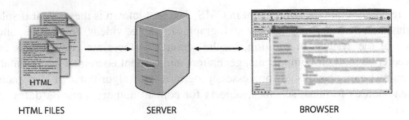

Fig. 3. Scheme of static websites [17]

Dynamic pages are generated in real-time in front of the HTML server based on data provided by the program to browse the Internet. These sites are dependent on the actions that the user is currently reviewing. For example, when you add a comment on the page, a new entry, date added and author appears. Sometimes additional user identifiers such as IP, the browser from which the page is displayed, and the version of the system are also provided. There are two ways to change content: First, the client-side uses scripting languages such as JavaScript and ActionScript that make direct changes to the Document Object Model (DOM) elements. The main advantages of this method are the shorter response times, the much less server load and the better interactive effect of the application. There is no need to contact the database, which is a big help in changing the code. The second method is the so-called. Server-side, using programming languages such as PHP, ASP and Perl. This processing is useful for database contact and persistent memory. An example of this activity is user validation or data exchange (Fig. 4).

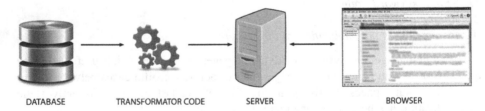

Fig. 4. Scheme of dynamic websites [17]

A content management system is a software that allows user to create, manage, and publish content. The early use of CMSs was mainly about managing documents and files, usually internally, and now it is managing the content on the public network. The purpose of such systems is to provide an intuitive interface for viewing user content as well as an interface for the site administrator, usually from the admin panel. CMSs are a great way to work with your system [18]:

A. *Dynamic content.*
B. *Easy to make changes.*
C. *Content Management Tab.*

D. *Add interactive content.*
E. *Integration with the media.*
F. *Full control over the entire site.*
G. *Allow many people to manage the site.*

Content Management Systems can fully support the knowledge management area in organizations. Currently, most of the free platforms are geared towards publishing content on the Internet. In the case of system installation on the local server, it is possible to support processes taking place on the premises of the organization. The system can be considered as the core of an organization that will aggregate all data and support internal communication. The next chapter is an analysis of the implementation of content management systems and its impact on the potential elimination of barriers in the knowledge management process between employees and organizational units.

4   Methods for Barrier Limitations in the Knowledge Management Process Using CMS

Enterprise content management processes have a direct impact on knowledge management. They support processes from the technological point of view. The author noted that implementing a CMS in an enterprise might translate into a partial elimination of communication and technological barriers to knowledge management in an organization.

In the case of individual barriers, a varied level of experience and knowledge can be standardized in the system. Aggregation of information and data at the server level will allow access to all employees regardless of their experience and seniority.

By empowering and attributing individual employees, the system can motivate to upload knowledge as one of the tasks of the daily schedule.

This can make employees aware of their level of knowledge. Age and gender differences and other externalities are automatically abolished. Managers can support the CMS to improve the overall management process as well. Systems can publish content for teams and supervise work performed by individual organizational units within a company. Through the systems can therefore be strengthened supervision of employees. Extensions that coordinate the task time can have the functionality of sending divert alerts. Discussing this topic should mention the possibility of using the core of system and thousands of plugins included in the system. The GNU GPL-based system allows modifications to the code made by thousands of developers around the world. User can also create his own extensions depending on how he use them. For example, for advanced medical companies, it is possible to create a register of medicines and patients, as well as conducting Business Intelligence analyzes, and for law firms, a directory of lawyers and online clients. Systems, whatever the industry, can support knowledge management in a given thematic area.

In a single process in the enterprise can be engaged a multitude of employees. The process can take place on the basis of equality or hierarchization. Below is an example process of system hierarchy [19, 20] (Fig. 5).

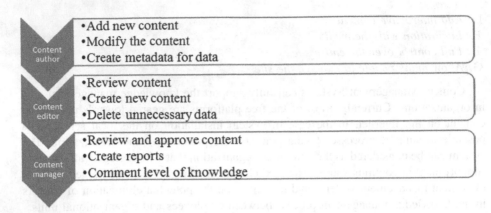

Fig. 5. Roles in hierarchical CMS distribution.

5 Conclusion

Implementation of Content Management Systems in the organization can improve the flow of information within the company, remove barriers to the exchange of knowledge between employees and increase efficiency and productivity of organizational units. The author noted the lack of literature indicating the possibility of using such systems in companies. By verifying the market, most organizations use paid platforms that are not standardized and do not have a common system. This article identifies specific systems that, thanks to the open source GNU GPL license, can be supported by thousands of free worldwide programs. Using an enterprise knowledge management system will increase company profits, employee productivity and creativity, and improve co-workers' relationships, and can also have an impact on improving managerial-level management accuracy as well as individual, organizational and technological barriers in many cases will be reduced.

References

1. Bergeron, B.: Essentials of Knowledge Management (2003)
2. Weichbroth, P., Brodnicki, K.: The lemniscate knowledge flow model. In: 2017 Federated Conference on Computer Science and Information Systems (FedCSIS), pp. 1217–1220. IEEE (2017)
3. Owoc, M., Weichbroth, P., Żuralski, K.: Towards better understanding of context-aware knowledge transformation. In: Computer Science and Information Systems (FedCSIS 2017), pp. 1123–1126. IEEE (2017)
4. J. Roy. Soc. Med. **94** (2001)
5. Owoc, M., Weichbroth, P.: Validation model for discovered web user navigation patterns. In: Mercier-Laurent, E., Boulanger, D. (eds.) AI4KM 2012. IAICT, vol. 422, pp. 38–52. Springer, Heidelberg (2014). https://doi.org/10.1007/978-3-642-54897-0_3

6. Weichbroth, P., Owoc, M., Pleszkun, M.: Web user navigation patterns discovery from WWW server log files. In: Computer Science and Information Systems (FedCSIS 2012), pp. 1171–1176. IEEE (2012)
7. Ossowska, K., Szewc, L., Weichbroth, P., Garnik, I., Sikorski, M.: Exploring an ontological approach for user requirements elicitation in the design of online virtual agents. In: Wrycza, S. (ed.) SIGSAND/PLAIS 2016. LNBIP, vol. 264, pp. 40–55. Springer, Cham (2016). https://doi.org/10.1007/978-3-319-46642-2_3
8. Weichbroth, P.: Delivering usability in IT products: empirical lessons from the field. Int. J. Softw. Eng. Knowl. Eng. 28(07), 1027–1045 (2018)
9. Mercier-Laurent, E., Jakubczyc, J., Owoc, M.L.: What is Knowledge Management? Prace Naukowe Akademii Ekonomicznej we Wrocławiu, Wroclaw, no. 815, pp. 9–21 (1999)
10. Redlarski, K., Weichbroth, P.: Hard lessons learned: delivering usability in IT projects. In: 2016 Federated Conference on Computer Science and Information Systems (FedCSIS), pp. 1379–1382. IEEE (2016)
11. Hauke, K., Owoc, M.L., Pondel, M.: Building data mining models in the Oracle 9i environment. In: Proceedings of Informing Science and IT Education (2003)
12. Pondel, M.: Business intelligence as a service in a cloud environment. In: Computer Science and Information Systems (FedCSIS 2013), pp. 1281–1283 IEEE (2013)
13. Hernes, M., Bytniewski, A.: Towards big management. In: Król, D., Nguyen, N.T., Shirai, K. (eds.) ACIIDS 2017. SCI, vol. 710, pp. 197–209. Springer, Cham (2017). https://doi.org/10.1007/978-3-319-56660-3_18
14. Hey, J.: The Data, Information, Knowledge. Wisdom Chain: The Metaphorical link (2004)
15. Boiko, B.: Content Management Bible (2005)
16. Mehta, N.: Choosing an Open Source CMS (2009)
17. Przysucha, Ł.: Content management systems based on GNU GPL license as a support of knowledge management in organizations and business. In: Mercier-Laurent, E., Boulanger, D. (eds.) AI4KM 2015. IAICT, vol. 497, pp. 51–65. Springer, Cham (2016). https://doi.org/10.1007/978-3-319-55970-4_4
18. Mehta, N.: Choosing an Open Source CMS. Beginner's Guide (2009)
19. Pondel, M., Korczak, J.: A view on the methodology of analysis and exploration of marketing data. In: Computer Science and Information Systems (FedCSIS 2017), pp. 1135–1143. IEEE (2017)
20. Pondel, M., Pondel, J.: Big Data solutions in cloud environment. In: FedCSIS Position Papers, pp. 233–238 (2016)

Selected It Tools in Enterprise Knowledge Management Processes – Overview and Efficiency Study

Maciej Pondel[1](✉) (iD) and Jolanta Pondel[2](✉) (iD)

[1] Wrocław University of Economics, Komandorska 118/120, Wrocław, Poland
maciej.pondel@ue.wroc.pl
[2] WSB University in Wrocław, Fabryczna St. 29-31, 53-609 Wrocław, Poland
jolanta.pondel@wsb.wroclaw.pl

Abstract. Today enterprises work in a rapidly changing environment. Those changes bring uncertainty about future that can result in high risks but also in new business opportunities. Modern communication technologies enable a better management of information and knowledge flows, what is essential to achieve a success in business. Digitalization processes experienced by modern companies require improvement of communication processes and knowledge management. This paper elaborates the essence of communication in modern companies. It overviews available IT tools supporting communication and knowledge management in enterprise. The aim of this article is to assess the current level of use of IT tools supporting knowledge management, by the companies considered as leaders in Poland, so the last part of the paper presents results of a survey research concerning usage, expectations and evaluation of available tools in Polish companies.

Keywords: Communication · IT communication tools · Enterprise social · Self-service business intelligence · Knowledge management

1 Introduction

It is vital for every business to attract top-quality employees because the potential of human resources determines the potential of the whole enterprise. Currently, employees are digitally and globally oriented, they expect diversity, and they are eager to participate in social media. At the same time, market expectations, customer's and client's needs and business requirements evolve faster than ever before. Enterprises may perceive change in terms of business challenges or opportunities. Those changes force an execution of necessary personnel changes. In this aspect companies can organize, create, implement platforms, processes and tools that will streamline processes. Technological development and communication solutions often allow better communication and more efficient corporate knowledge management. Initially, modern technological solutions caused much controversy. Organizations primarily were afraid of uncontrolled spread of information and low security of information. Enterprises were accustomed to full control of communication processes but they noted that in the age of

© IFIP International Federation for Information Processing 2019
Published by Springer Nature Switzerland AG 2019
E. Mercier-Laurent and D. Boulanger (Eds.): AI4KM 2017, IFIP AICT 571, pp. 12–28, 2019.
https://doi.org/10.1007/978-3-030-29904-0_2

mobility, BYOD and social networks they can lose efficiency and employee engagement, which has led them to take advantage of modern communication platforms.

Communication is most commonly performed by the Internet and the services Internet offers. According to literature, 615 million Europeans regularly use Internet. Taking into account 2000–2016, the growth of Internet users in Europe is 485,2%. The number of people using the Internet worldwide is already 3,675 billion. However, despite the fact that these values are very high and seems promising (given the popularity of using Internet communication technologies), there are still areas in the world that are cut off from the Internet and some of its services, such as the Web 2.0 or mobile services. According to sources only about 50,1% of the global population actively use the Internet [1].

First section of this paper elaborates the essence of communication and knowledge management in enterprises. Next section covers the types of communication in companies. Third chapter elaborates the requirements regarding communication system in companies and presents typology of communication tools. Following section overviews available IT tools supporting communication and knowledge management. Last chapter introduces the result of a survey research regarding usage, expectations and evaluation of available tools in Polish companies.

2 The Essence of Communication and Knowledge Management in Enterprises

The competitiveness of an enterprise depends on the skills and involvement of employees, which is related to the access of information and knowledge and exchange of information between management, employees, customers, etc. Effective communication and the flow of information and knowledge enable the proper functioning of people and teams and it motivates to work.

Word communication "communication" (lat.) – connection, other meanings in different languages are message, commonality [2]. In other words communication means exchanging information between two or more people (employees).

In literature, the process of effective communication means "sending a message in such a way that the message received is as close as possible to the intended message" [3], "a process in which people strive to share meaning through symbolic messages (messages)" [4]. The purpose of communication is shaping, modification, change of knowledge, attitudes, behaviors, indications, suggestions of ways of acting. Efficient communication is crucial to achieve proper knowledge management in organization. The objective of Knowledge Management System is to support creation, transfer, and application of knowledge in organizations [5].

Communication and knowledge management in an enterprise are recognized as a fundamental factor of proper company functioning, because it is closely linked to the management of the enterprise. Effective communication is essential for executives to set up tasks, plans, communicate information to employees, etc., while employees provide their own views on the activities, plans, accomplishing the tasks, communicating with the clients. Communication allows each other to interact with others, and depending on the skills may be stronger or weaker, faster or slower. It is worth mentioning that business communication is usually directly linked to the core management functions, i.e. planning, organizing, motivating and controlling, and executing those functions through the communication process.

Mintzberg pointed out 3 types of managerial roles related to communication [4]:

1. interpersonal - connector, representative, leader communicating with subordinates, customers, suppliers and colleagues in the organization,
2. information - monitor, spokesman disseminating information on tasks, work, duties, provide information about the enterprise, department as a whole,
3. decision-making - negotiator, entrepreneur, implementing new projects, resolving conflicts, allocating resources, tasks.

3 Types of Communication in Enterprises

An effective communication process plays an important role in the company's performance and effectiveness. Employees performing tasks in collaboration create specific relationships, influence others' behavior, convey information and knowledge, and enforce certain values, norms, and patterns of behavior. Effective communication enables the development of employees through the exchange of knowledge and experience. It helps them to better understand the assigned tasks and expectations regarding the way of implementation and execution.

Communication in the enterprise can be divided in regards to [6, 7]:

- Flow direction:
    1. vertical - exchange of information between employees and supervisors (between different levels of management);
    2. horizontal - exchange of information between members of the same team or persons performing the same function.

- Nature of information transmission:
    1. formal - resulting from the organizational structure of the company,
    2. informal - formed on the basis of informal relationships between employees.

- Message type:
    1. private - sent to friends for informal purposes (not related to official duties);
    2. business (but not public) - their purpose is to inform the recipient about work related matters,
    3. public - sent to many people directly and simultaneously.

- Nature of the interaction:
    1. direct - exchange of information directly, usually intended to trigger specific activities,
    2. indirect - the transmission of information not directly when additional individuals, means of communication, technical devices are involved.

- Scope of impact:

  1. between the company and the environment - exchange of information, between employees and outsiders,
  2. inside the company - exchange of information between members of the enterprise,
  3. interpersonal communication - exchange of information between its participants.

- Information flow in communication networks:

  1. centralized communication - facilitates solving simple problems, usually indicated by procedures (not too effective for solving complex problems);
  2. decentralized communication - takes into account the real needs and capabilities of employees, facilitates solving more complex tasks.

The basis for communication is to reach and manage useful information, so the form, the way, the timing of the transfer of relevant information, and the use of decision-making information are of great importance. Depending on what to whom, when you want to be communicated, you need to select the right communication channel, and the use of a specific form of communication affects how the recipient reacts to the message.

4 Enterprise Communication System

Enterprise successes on the market when it fulfills its mission, the quality of the products and services it offers is satisfactory, the company has a reputation for being credible, it has a well-established market position, and makes the desired profit. Success depends on many factors. One of them is the right communication and knowledge management both inside and outside the enterprise.

Well-planned communication system in the enterprise creates the opportunity of [8, 9]:

- increase work efficiency,
- problems identification,
- finding ways to solve problems,
- increase employee involvement and loyalty,
- raising overall motivation for work and organizational culture,
- improving people-to-people relationships and understanding,
- understanding the needs of change and reduce resistance to change,
- creating values relevant for the proper development of the company.

Introduced, modified communication system in the company should.

- take into account information and knowledge needs of employees,
- establish key communication areas (of particular importance to the company, resulting in expected employee attitudes, identify the purpose and forms of communication);

- distinguish employees/teams according to the scope of information needs and adapt them to forms of communication,
- establish rules for checking the effectiveness of processes, communication tools and their impact on the functioning of an enterprise.

Businesses collect more and more data and information for problem solving and decision-making processes, both in operational and strategic areas. This would not be possible without the use of information technology, information and knowledge management, and the use of specific IT tools to streamline the process. The effectiveness of the tasks performed and the decisions made is influenced by, among others, the ability to appropriately select IT tools for communication, sources of information, speed of acquisition, processing of information and knowledge. Properly chosen tools for communication and knowledge management help you make the most accurate decision in the shortest possible time, with low risk.

Contemporary enterprise electronic communication tools include:

- Intranet (extranet),
- Email,
- Instant Messaging/chat,
- Audioconference/teleconference,
- Videoconference with desktop sharing,
- Corporate blog,
- Social networking (enterprise social),
- Enterprise wiki,
- Individual and group calendar,
- Document management system,
- Task management systems,
- Business intelligence system for creating and sharing management dashboards.

5   Examples of Communication and Knowledge Management Tools in Enterprise

Efficient communication platform in modern enterprise should enable employees:

- Collaboration,
    - Content/Information publishing
    - Social networking
    - Real time communication
- Task and goals assignment and they further discussions/clarification,
- Document management,
- Information search,
- Workflow management,
- Reporting, analyses and insights sharing.

Collaboration software is designed to improve productivity of individuals, teams and organizations. This is achieved through the following capabilities of collaboration software (see [10]):

- informing,
- coordinating,
- actually collaborating,
- cooperating.

Examples of collaboration software are:

- In terms of content and information management:
  - Liferay,
  - Atlassian Confluence,
  - Microsoft SharePoint being presented in Fig. 1.

Fig. 1. Example of MS Sharepoint site

- In terms of social networking
  - Yammer being presented in Fig. 2,
  - Slack,
  - IBM's Connections.
- In terms of real time communication
  - Atlassian HipChat,
  - Skype For Business,
  - Jabber.

Fig. 2. Example of Yammer home page.

Tasks and goals assignment to employees and execution progress tracking can be supported by an **issue tracking system (ITS).** It is a software application that allows enterprise to record and follow the progress of every task or a problem or "issue" that a team member identifies, until the problem is resolved. With an ITS, an "issue", which can be anything from a simple customer question to a detailed technical report of an error or bug or even a goal to achieved by employee (useful in Management by Objectives approach). Issue can be tracked by priority status, owner or some other customized criteria.

An ITS provides the user with a way to report an issue, track progression towards its resolution, and know who is responsible for task competition. It also allows the manager of the system to customize the tracking procedure so that unnecessary documentation on the part of the problem solvers does not become a waste of time. Many kinds of enterprises use ITS applications, including software developers, manufacturers, IT help desks, and other service providers [11].

Examples of such applications are:

- Atlassian Jira,
- Trello,
- Redmine,
- Microsoft Office 365 Planner – presented in Fig. 3.

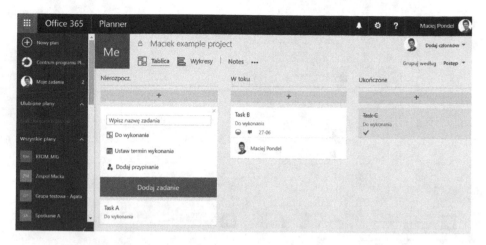

Fig. 3. Example of Microsoft Office Planner application

Workflow systems are considered mainly as tools supporting business processes. A workflow application implements a business process model. The model describes the process steps to be performed to achieve a specific business goal, business rules for coordination of those steps and responsibilities of process participants [12]. The steps include tasks that should be performed by agents that can be human, computer systems or combination of both [13]. Workflow systems, with the benefits of efficient and flexible process modelling and process automation, have been widely used for managing business processes. Communication and knowledge management processes are very often treated as a small processes that should be executed according to the business rules defined in a workflow tool e.g.:

- Document approvals - business rules define who is responsible for creation and approval of documents. Every kind of document can have individual list of approvers.
- Change management – the workflow can define how the change should be identified, described, estimated and who should be responsible for its approval and execution.
- Risk management – the workflow can enforce the specified risk description by a project manager and can lead the process of execution of preventive actions.
- And many more.

There are many software applications enabling workflow automation. Usually they provide user with Graphical User Interface where users can model the process and then the flows are executed. An example process automation application MS Flow is presented in Fig. 4. One can observe there a modelling feature of the application that allows building process by selecting "boxes" representing actions and connecting them in order to reflect business rules. The main advantages of such applications are:

- Increasing productivity of employees,
- Ability to measure to productivity,
- Precise execution of business functions (in accordance with the assumed process).

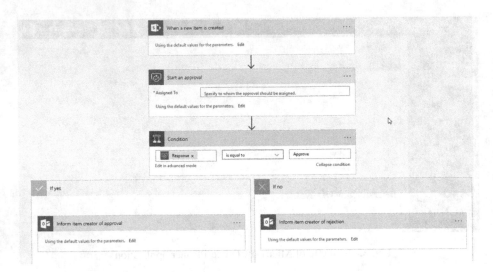

Fig. 4. Example of Microsoft Flow application

Reporting and analyses are essential when we would like to control and monitor all aspects of the company. We use Business Intelligence tools that could integrate the data from all the systems used in a company to present the holistic reports. Regarding Business Intelligence tools we can distinguish.

- Traditional BI based on ETL process, data warehouses, data marts, OLAP, dashboards, scorecards and analytics.
- Self Sevice BI where Power Users connect to various data sources and create their data models on which they build visualisation layer.

Examples of most common Self Service Business Intelligence tools are:

- Microsoft Power BI,
- Tableau,
- QlikView.

Power BI is a Microsoft developed suite that belong to the group of tools called Self Service BI. Of course the main goal of such tool is to provide Business Intelligence capability but the difference expressed in Self-service boils down to the fact that in this tool the final user (accountant, analyst, manager and many other) is capable to build their own analysis (data models, reports, dashboards) with only limited assistance of the IT department (see [14]).

Also, it's important to emphasize that there are two kinds of self-serve BI user (see [15]):

- Analytics Power Users who create visual apps from multiple data sources – both internal and external.
- Regular Users that can fully explore the visual apps created by power users or IT.

Power BI is a cloud-based business analytics service that provides user with the most important BI features like creating rich interactive reports with Power BI Desktop and monitoring the health of business using live dashboards. It includes 2 main approaches to analyse data:

- Power BI Desktop,
- Power BI for Office 365.

Power BI desktop is a free desktop tool in which you can (see [16]):

- Import.
  You can import data from a wide variety of data sources. After user connects to a data source, he or she can shape the data before importing to match analysis and reporting needs.
- Model data.
  Power BI Desktop provides data modelling features like autodetect and manual relationships definition, custom measures, calculated columns, data categorization, and sort by column. There is Relationship View, where user gets a customizable diagram view of all tables and the relationships between them.

Power BI for Office 365 is a cloud based service available via web browser that allows (see [16]):

- Execution of similar report creation process like in Power BI Desktop (import, model, create report).
- Connect to services.
  User is able to connect to content packs for a number of services such as Salesforce, Microsoft Dynamics, and Google Analytics. Power BI uses user's credentials to connect to the service, and then creates a Power BI dashboard and a set of Power BI reports that automatically show data and provide visual insights.
- Create Dashboards.
  They are personalized and provide user capability to monitor most important data, at a glance. A dashboard combines on-premises and cloud data in a single, consolidated view across the organization.
  Sharing the data. In Power BI user can share dashboards, reports, and tiles in several different ways e.g. Publish a report to the web, share a dashboard with associates, create a dashboard in a group, then share it with co-workers outside the group.
- Q&A in Power BI.
  Capability of processing natural language user's question and receive answers in the form of charts and graphs.
- Quick Insights.
  Power BI searches different subsets of dataset while applying a set of algorithms to discover potentially-interesting insights. Power BI scans as much of a dataset as possible in an allotted amount of time. Example algorithms are: Majority, Category outliers, Overall trends in time series, Correlation and many more.

6   Research on Usage of Communication and Knowledge Management Tools on Enterprises

Authors have conducted research to verify how IT tools affect communication in Polish companies, which tools are most popular and where those companies identify the most important advantages. The essence of the study was to determine the direction of development of communication tools used by enterprises. The survey was addressed to employees of IT, HR, corporate communications, and was implemented using a combined method: online surveys and telephone interviews. The basic tool used in the study was an anonymous survey directed to employees of enterprises of various lines of business. Those companies were selected on the basis of rankings of enterprises published by Polish business magazines, in which the use of communication solutions is necessary for proper functioning.

A group of 100 companies was selected for the survey.

Regarding the size of the companies that took part in the survey, the majority (60%) were medium enterprises, employing between 50 and 249 employees and making an annual turnover not exceeding EUR 50 million. Another group was large companies operating in one country. This group accounted for 34%. The survey covered 6% of the companies referred to as corporations (operating in many countries) –Fig. 5.

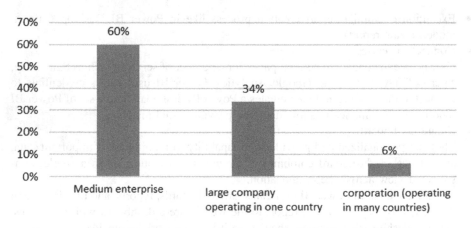

Fig. 5. Number of companies in research divided by the size.

The respondents were asked to evaluate how the use of IT tools in communication affects specific activities (Table 1). Authors assigned specific weight to each answer, they calculated values and then ranked answers. Respondents pointed out that the use of IT tools for communication speeds up the communication process (rank 1) and enables to perform more effectively the assigned tasks (rank 2). It also influences the creation and consolidation of the positive image of the company. Encouraging employees to communicate was ranked in the lowest position of the indicated actions. It transpires that simply putting IT tools into communication does not make employees to increase contact frequency or they prefer personal contacts.

Table 1. Impact of IT tools on selected communication process activities

Communication process using IT tools	Weight					Total weight	Ranking
	5	4	3	2	1		
	Rating						
	Definitely yes	Rather yes	Hard to say	Rather no	Definitely no		
It affects employee behavior and attitudes in relation to customers	19	38	37	5	1	14562	5
Creates and maintains a positive image of the company	16	56	27	1	0	18003	3
Encourages employees to communicate (internally and externally)	4	38	51	7	0	3207	6
Allows employees to provide specific information	13	60	22	5	0	15676	4
Speeds up communication	64	31	3	2	0	39693	1
It allows for better performance of tasks	37	40	20	3	0	29666	2

The respondents were asked to evaluate the effectiveness of the indicated communication tools (Table 2). The highest rating got email (1st place). As many as 94 respondents indicated that this is a very important/important communication tool in enterprises. This is probably due to its popularity, versatility regarding the type of message delivery, time, size and cost of implementation, maintenance, updates. On 2nd place there is intranet/extranet - with 75 important and very important answers. This tool, because of its cost, is not used by all companies, however, in the research it has gained a high position, probably due to its usefulness and development potential. Audio and videoconferencing go places 3 and 4 in the ranking. 5th place take company wikis as a tool playing an important role in the communication process. It is a tool that complements the knowledge of employees and develops as needed, enables teamwork, facilitates the management of large amounts of information, and provides the ability to create knowledge bases and share them with the business environment.

The results confirm that communication and knowledge management is very important for businesses. IT tools play an important role in improving the efficiency and effectiveness of activities, transferring and gathering content (including knowledge), and therefore business leaders should be aware that well-functioning communication can enable achieving the goals.

Table 2. Evaluation of the importance of IT communication tools

Tool category	Weight					Total weight	Ranking
	5	4	3	2	1		
	Significance						
	Very important	Important	Medium important	Less important	Not important		
Email	**51**	43	6	0	0	445	**1**
Company wiki	10	23	19	24	24	271	5
Intranet (extranet)	11	64	23	2	0	384	2
Enterprise blog	0	3	8	53	36	178	**9**
Videoconference	0	27	39	30	4	289	4
Newsletter	6	11	40	29	14	266	6
Audio conference	0	35	45	20	0	315	3
Enterprise social	3	20	14	47	16	247	7
Instant messaging	3	4	28	37	28	217	8
Others	0	0	23	17	**60**	163	10

As part of the research work, authors have decided to check the level of communication efficiency. Respondents were requested to evaluate each individual element impacting the overall communication efficiency.

Table 3 summarizes the results. As in previous analyses weights have been assigned to specific answers and the summarized values have been calculated. Then the results were divided by the number of respondents and an average value was calculated for each area. Over a half of the respondents (51) assess as good and very good the reliability and completeness of the information received (mean 3.37). A similar number of respondents (48) highly evaluate efficient access to information (average 3.31). The speed of information flow was also considered as high (average 3.26) and the communication atmosphere - average 3.24. IT tools significantly speed up the process of processing access to information. The lowest rated elements were "the amount of information received with reference to information needs" (average 3.22) and the "relevance of communication activities with the needs of employees" (average grade 3.18). The ideal situation would be if the amount and type of information needed was equal to the amount received. Such situation is of course very difficult to achieve. The latter aspect got the most negative answers (23). It is necessary to pay attention to communication activities in enterprises. The reason of negative ratings may be wrong tools, inability to use them in a correct way or mismatch between expected and executed methods of communication. The reason for the generally low results of the study may be a large number of people indicating the answer "hard to say". The results are shown in Table 3.

In the next question, the respondents were requested to assess the influence of communication tools on the group work behaviours. Group/team work was understood as cooperation of employees in the execution of the assigned tasks.

As earlier, respondents were asked to rate each category on a 5-point scale. Method of the final rating calculation was the same as in previous case. The results are presented in Table 3.

Table 3. Evaluation of elements impacting the communication supported by ICT efficiency.

Element of communication efficiency	Weight					Average value	Ranking
	5	4	3	2	1		
	Rating						
	Definitely yes	Rather yes	Hard to say	Rather no	Definitely no		
The reliability and completeness of the information received	6	45	31	16	2	**3,37**	1
Efficient access to information	6	42	33	15	4	3,31	2
Speed of information flow	7	41	30	15	7	3,26	3
Communication atmosphere	5	38	38	14	5	3,24	4
The amount of information received with reference to information needs	4	40	34	18	4	3,22	5
Relevance of communication activities with the needs of employees	6	33	38	19	4	**3,18**	6

Respondents assessed that the main reason of using ICT in team and group work is the exchange of experience/knowledge, better results during collaborative work on a task and easier common goal achievement, however, it should be noted that effective performance of tasks in the team is possible due to the appropriate tasks' division between team members. The advantage of team work is not only to facilitate the implementation of tasks through their division, but also to increase productivity, resulting from the fact that the integrated group is more effective in action than individual who is part of a team and communication tools streamline the information and knowledge flow in teams. In subsequent places, we can find the following categories: "to reduce stress and increase creativity", "increase work efficiency", "increase motivation (social facilitation)", "higher sense of responsibility", "obtain faster effects". These activities are related to human traits and have been indicated as significant (average rating of the activities listed from 3.74 to 3.02). When creating teams, remember to develop an evaluation system and inform about the applicable rules/criteria all team members before starting their work. The rating of the effects of the group's activities and the contribution of the work of individual people is an extremely difficult task, which is why it must be prepared in detail and verified before the introduction. Collective responsibility should not be used because the team's individual work as well as the entire team and they are assessed as part of the team. During the team's work there may also be conflicts, or situations in which a conflict of interests arose, and its participants try to impose their will on each other. In group work such an event should be solved as soon as possible to prevent their escalation, which will make the whole team's work difficult. Good methods are negotiation and compromise (Table 4).

Table 4. Influence of communication tools on the group work behaviours

	Weight					Average value	Ranking
	5	4	3	2	1		
	Rating						
	Definitely yes	Rather yes	Hard to say	Rather no	Definitely no		
Exchange of experience/knowledge	41	38	19	2	0	4,18	1
Better results	36	40	20	4	0	4,08	2
A common goal achievement	39	29	29	3	0	4,04	3
To reduce stress and increase creativity	16	48	30	6	0	3,74	4
Increase work efficiency	16	45	32	5	2	3,68	5
Increase motivation (social facilitation)	8	36	45	11	0	3,41	6
Higher sense of responsibility	11	29	47	13	0	3,38	7
Obtain faster effects	12	38	27	21	2	3,37	8

7 Conclusions

In current times we have a variety of tools supporting communication and knowledge management. Some of them are easy accessible even for small companies due to the fact that they are available as a service and require only subscription fee to be covered and no huge upfront investments are necessary.

As it transpires from the research, the variety of communication tools does not solve all the communication problems in current enterprises. Employees have a lot of communication tools and channels but at the same time they can suffer from the low level of information relevance or too high amount of information they receive with reference with their actual needs.

Every business should care about high quality communication. Effective communication has the impact on increasing trust in the organization and supporting organizational culture. Well informed employees are more motivated to work better. Without proper communication, the involvement of the staff is low and in extreme cases even the lack of understanding can be experienced. For tasks requiring personal involvement of the employee and his invention, lack of knowledge or understanding of the goal may lead to wrong decisions. At the same time, thanks to their knowledge, employees communicate well with the environment and they convey the right information about the company and its activities.

References

1. Internetworldstats 2017, World Internet Usage And Population Statistics. http://www.internetworldstats.com/stats.htm
2. Mała, N., Hrabelska, O.: Informacja i komunikacja w zarządzaniu personelem. Nierówności społeczne a wzrost gospodarczy (36), 317–326 (2013)
3. Griffin, R.W., Rusinski, M., Rozanska, I.: Podstawy zarzadzania organizacjami; Przekl. M. Rusinski; Konsultacja nauk. B. Glinski; Red. I. Rozanska. Warszawa: Wydaw. Nauk. PWN (1999)
4. Stoner, J.A.F., Freeman, R.E., Gilbert Jr, D.R.: Kierowanie, wydanie II. Wydawnictwo PWE, Warszawa (2001)
5. Alavi, M., Leidner, D.E.: Knowledge management and knowledge management systems: conceptual foundations and research issues. MIS Q. 107–136 (2001)
6. Stankiewicz, J.: Komunikowanie się w organizacji. Astrum, Wrocław (2006)
7. Muszyńska, K.: Zarządzanie komunikacją w projekcie w wybranych metodykach zarządzania projektami. Studia i Materiały Polskiego Stowarzyszenia Zarządzania Wiedzą 17, 131–138 (2008)
8. O'Hair, D., Friedrich, G.W., Dixon, L.D.: Strategic Communication in Business and the Professions. Allyn & Bacon (2007)
9. Czekaj, J.: Metody zarządzania informacją w przedsiębiorstwie. Zeszyty Naukowe/Akademia Ekonomiczna w Krakowie. Seria Specjalna, Monografie (143) (2000)
10. Hildenbrand, T., Rothlauf, F., Geisser, M., Heinzl, A., Kude, T.: Approaches to collaborative software development. In: 2008 International Conference on Complex, Intelligent and Software Intensive Systems, pp. 523–528. IEEE, March 2008
11. Techtarget: Issue tracking system (ITS) definition (2015). http://searchcrm.techtarget.com/definition/issue-tracking-system
12. Schmidt, M.T.: Building workflow business objects. In: Patel, D., Sutherland, J., Miller, J. (eds.) Business Object Design and Implementation II, pp. 64–76. Springer, London (1998). https://doi.org/10.1007/978-1-4471-1286-0_8

13. Demeyer, R., Van Assche, M., Langevine, L., Vanhoof, W.: Declarative workflows to efficiently manage flexible and advanced business processes. In: Proceedings of the 12th International ACM SIGPLAN Symposium on Principles and Practice of Declarative Programming, pp. 209–218. ACM, July 2010
14. Webb, C.: Power Query for Power BI and Excel. Apress (2014)
15. Owoc, M., Pondel, M.: Selection of free software useful in business intelligence. Teaching methodology perspective. In: Mercier-Laurent, E., Boulanger, D. (eds.) AI4KM 2016. IAICT, vol. 518, pp. 93–105. Springer, Cham (2018). https://doi.org/10.1007/978-3-319-92928-6_6
16. Power BI Desktop (2016). https://powerbi.microsoft.com/en-us/documentation

Selected Knowledge Management Aspects in Modern Education

Katarzyna Hołowińska[✉]

Wroclaw University of Economics,
Komandorska 118/120, 53-345 Wroclaw, Poland
katarzyna.holowinska@ue.wroc.pl

Abstract. Modern organizations are challenged to permanently be prepared for changes. The competitive advantage can be reached only when organizations are aware what resources are the most essential for the proper functioning. This situation is linked also to the modern education which nowadays have to be more market oriented. Such approach requires greater involvement and allows faster development, thanks to competitiveness which naturally stimulates activity. The main goal of the article is to present new approaches of modern teaching in context of KM. The first part presents roots of KM and it's definition. The second part is connected with challenges of modern education. The last section describes KM tools used as an aspects of present education.

Keywords: Knowledge management · Modern education · KM tools

1 Introduction

Dynamic continuous development of Knowledge Management (KM) is expanding in new fields like education and caused huge change in this area. Using new technologies, elements of artificial intelligence, complex systems, etc. leads to market oriented organizations including Universities. Efficient KM systems implemented within universities can provide the information about present trends in the jobs market, economy both levels global and local, but also the knowledge accumulated by the university itself and the finest practices of the world best universities. Applying KM on universities can deliver decision support tool which may be connected with broad activities like teaching, research or management [1]. The article presents the description of KM roots and answering the question about what are the tools which can be used in effective KM used in university environment.

Undoubtedly the basic objective of Knowledge Management is extending the innovation capacity of organizations by better use of knowledge, talents or opportunities and technologies. Obviously it is not easy to apply KM mainly because it needs certain change of attitude, like listening instead of push, collaborating not competing, gathering, sharing experiences and evaluating the benefits.

Published by Springer Nature Switzerland AG 2019
E. Mercier-Laurent and D. Boulanger (Eds.): AI4KM 2017, IFIP AICT 571, pp. 29–39, 2019.
https://doi.org/10.1007/978-3-030-29904-0_3

2 Knowledge Management as a Natural Way of PostIndustrial Changes

The sociological and economical changes which took place recently were connected with transformation from traditional industrial era linked to the traditional values like capital, land and work to new era linked with knowledge where the information is the core resource and determine the competitive advantage on the market. All this changes lead to development of new branch of management the idea of knowledge management. The table below presents the differences between attitudes in industry era and knowledge era. The difference between approaches are diametrically in basic fields in organization (Table 1).

Table 1. Comparison of industry era and knowledge era (Source: own elaboration, based on: M. Strojny, Teoria i praktyka zarządzania wiedzą, "Ekonomika i Organizacja Przedsiębiorstwa", 2000)

	Industry era	Knowledge era
Basic resource	Capital	Knowledge
People (employees)	Cost	Investment
Authority	It depends on position in structure of the organization	It depends on skills and knowledge
Management style	Injunctons and control	Participatory
Organizational structure	Hierarchical	Virtual, flat or hypertext
Strategy	Focused on competition	Focused on cooperation
Organizational culture	Based on obedience	Based on trust
Market value	Depends on financial and material assets	Depends on intellectual capital
Motivation	Financial incentives	Satisfaction incentives
Customer relationship	Unidirectional through the market	Interactive through collaboration
Continuous change	Threat	Opportunity
Development	Linear, predictable	Chaotic, hard to predict
Using new technologies	Important	Necessary
Dominant sector	Industry	Service, processing information
The most important invention	Assembly line	Internet
Leading companies	General Motors, Ford	Microsoft, Amazon

The fundamental element of growth is innovation, but there is no innovation without proper knowledge. With this intensive development of technologies there is a change from traditional approaches to those which use modern solutions to improve efficiency and competitive advantage. This change is also connected with education field which is so crucial for each society. The modern universities competing between each other and this situation shows new perspective. The universities can be perceived as a businesses.

Knowledge management can be considered in variety forms as a process, system, scientific discipline, new philosophy of management. KM can be simply defined as a doing what is needed to get the essence of knowledge resources. The beginnings of KM was applied to individuals but with the time it is turned out that it also can be used in context of organizations. With this huge amount of information which surrounded us everyday knowledge management is considered as very important discipline. Peter Drucker whom can be consider as a father of KM said, that the knowledge is the key resource and not only in context of economic strength but also as a nation's military strength, he highlighted that there is a need to work on the knowledge in quality and productivity levels. Undoubtedly nowadays the most essential resource of today's organization is the collective knowledge which stays in awareness of whole organizational environment like employees, customers or vendors. Understanding how to organize knowledge in modern enterprises gives many benefits like: developing the most important business competences, increase level of innovation, empowering workers, bringing high quality products to the market, developing time cycles and decision making and finally building strong competitive advantage [1].

The Institute of system production and projecting technologies in Berlin define KM as a set of methods, instruments and tools which have influence on progress of core business processes in context of knowledge which means generating, storage and distribution of knowledge at the same time with using the definition of knowledge aims and identification of the knowledge on all levels and fields of organization [2]. Stewart [2] understand KM as a having a knowledge about the knowledge of particular people, gaining this knowledge and organizing to use it to benefit.

It is possible to find more and more variety definitions of knowledge management but most of them have some common elements. Definitely the idea of knowledge management is based on three main processes: creating, sharing and using the knowledge. With those processes very important in knowledge management systems are: [3]

- technology (Internet, Intranet, Extranet, group work systems), which mean decision support systems or tools which are designed for individual needs
- systems, tools and methods of measuring effectiveness of using the knowledge
- organizational culture which is oriented on people and thanks to this, it is more common to share the knowledge.

Today the most important element of modern management is the knowledge in cooperation with technologies and using it in variety fields.

3 Challenges of Modern Education

Nowadays the access to even latest technology is not a problem caused most of them are intended for mass use, consequently the dynamic of expectations changed. We expect services to be delivered faster, with more modern methods best quality and price. And it is not just about business-related services but also services related to social aspects, progress or education. Especially the last one – education has changed recently. Thanks to the big competition between universities potential students are more like consumers and from this perspective they also making decisions related with education path. Universities rankings are growing in importance and have great influence on perception of universities on the international market. Today students searching services and education with access to new technologies and flexibility in offered options. To be competitive enough and to manage with this precise student expectations universities have to prepare modern facilities and special infrastructure but also new methods of sharing the knowledge. Knowledge Management field has more and more meaning in variety fields. As it turned out not only does it work in corporate business but also in other ground like education field [4].

The main approach in modern education should concentrate on student's individual activity, arrangement of self-learning conditions and useful practical training, but also the whole administration connected with education supposed to be available anytime, easy and reliable. These requirements have been reflected in new teaching methods like e-learning which begin to used not only as a support of classes but more often as a main technique of teaching. Because universities are complex institutions and the flow of knowledge is not only linked to the teaching the students but also with the administration and sharing the knowledge between other organizations that is why the KM tools like Intranets, Document Management, Project Management, Decision Support Systems etc. are so applicable and using them increase the effectiveness of the whole institution. Moreover such methods of teaching like flipping classroom, gamification, using social media or design thinking etc., begin to be more and more popular and seems to be perfect methods which meet requirements of modern education market. Furthermore it is impossible to find one perfect universal teaching method mainly because each student have different perception, and different methods fit to different people. In this case the best solution is the hybridization of few methods is the most effective way which suit especially the biggest groups of students [5].

4 Knowledge Management Aspects Connected with Permanent Learning/Education

Unquestionably Knowledge Management contributes to increase competitive advantage as a method of accumulating and proper sharing knowledge between people in whole environment of the organization. To support and control this process organizations may use special tools to organize particular modules of business core which can be used efficiently also in context of Knowledge Management in education [6].

E-learning

The dynamic growth of the Internet definitely have affected the process of learning. Till recently the growth was connected with business to business or business to consumer transactions. Nevertheless the growth of online learning meaning is increasing. According to estimations the learner to education transaction will be third most popular part of the Internet traffic. In addition the World Bank predicted that until 2020 about 90 million students will take part in making degrees or other shorter trainings by distance learning. The estimations of this market shows even more than $100 billion value [7].

Rosenberg defines e-learning as a using the Internet for delivering wide selection of solutions which improve knowledge and performance. It is grounded on three basic criteria and characteristic e-learning as a: [8]

• Networked which means that is capable of continuous updating/storing/recovering/ distributing and sharing information.
• Distributed to the end – user through the computer.
• Focused on the widest view of learning- learning explanations which go beyond the usual models of training.

Training based on the technology has been popular for many years, however the Internet increase the speed, proximity and interaction between learners and teachers. The development of e-learning caused measurable business benefits that can be used on an Intranet and Internet. According to Rosenberg the most important benefits of e-learning are: [8]

• reducing costs;
• improving business responsiveness;
• messages which are reliable and flexible with option to customizing;
• suitable and dependable content;
• unlimited time learning;
• universality;
• can be created by community;
• scaleability.

This change in learning methods will cause risks and opportunities for traditional education and definitely will be a new way for both learners and educators to cope with. Moreover this new paradigm of e-learning requires sometimes different structure and more modern, universal and global attitude. The main element which have influence on this change is technology. Furthermore the technology makes the process of learning more individual and interactive. Tapscott explained the change of interactive learning is a step from traditional one size for all learners to a modern attitude of learning which is customized and intended for the individual user. According to Tapscott traditional attitude of learning have been linear opposite to modern attitude which thanks to the Internet is more interactive and non-linear. Such non-linear learning mean that the user have full control over the learning process [8] (Fig. 1).

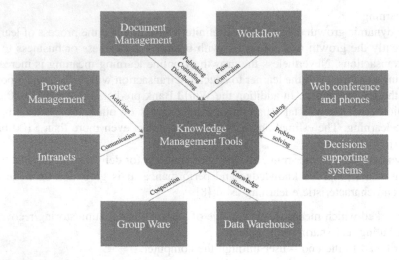

Fig. 1. Knowledge management tools. (Source: own elaboration, based on: A Tiwana Knowledge Management Toolkit)

- Document management

    Naturally universities have a lot of important information exist in paper form. That is why there is a need to change it into a more transferable and searchable electronic form by scanning. It is important to noticed that this action should not be considered as a Knowledge Management initiative. Sometimes converting and cataloging the most important information for the organization is simply sufficient. However using the tools which supporting versioning of the document during the teams working on documentation or creating new documents can be very helpful. This guarantee that all team members have access to the most updated version of particular document and it is helping to avoid working on inconsistent versions. Document management includes also capacity of developing the documents database and categorize them automatically. In such institution like university this kind of solution provide consistent and well maintained the policy of managing with documents in whole organization.

- Workflow

    The tools which support workflow in the organization allows users to easily make visualization and automatization of the current processes, but also gives possibility to monitor progress or even modify those processes in real time. This kind of tool is especially useful in environment like universities where appear many processes and projects which require some control to avoid chaos.

- Web conference and phones

    The phones and web conferences seems to fit perfect for the characteristic of effective knowledge management tool as an instrument which let to develop informal cooperation, discussion and chats. This tool appeared in following forms:

- Virtual meetings, give possibility for users in different localizations to connect, manage the meeting and share the information. In addition users have options to share applications in form of the screens, graphics, word processing or spreadsheets in real time.
- Document collaboration, let users to cooperate with all team members or other participants on variety forms of documents or programs in real time. The users not only can view shared information but can also take control of the shared programs and fill or edit some data there.
- Informal communication, it is also important to highlight that the chats may take place with natural voice and with the virtual presence. The academic research has shown that people who have possibility to see each other face to face create trust more easily.

All those proposals give chance to shorten the geographic distance as if it were not exist at all, and obviously it give great work effectiveness especially in such environment like educational institution.

- Decisions Supporting Systems

Those systems help to make minor and major decisions quick and correctly thanks to analysis of historical data and past experiences. Data mining instruments support in finding precise trends and patterns from data warehouses.

- Data Warehouse

A tool used in case when university is using multiplication of the databases which are existing in hierarchy and data warehouse uniform all of this databases. This tool provide possibility to use several different databases at the same time, merge their content, run queries at once or reduce data chaos. Because data warehouses collective and combine data from various sources and collect data in process this solution increase the quality of data.

- Group Ware

Obviously the process of making, distributing and using knowledge involves cooperation. Innovative activities based on knowledge are intensively cooperative. GroupWare instruments deliver document repository, remote integration and ground for cooperative work.

- Intranets

Availability of the information capital inside and outside a university gives possibility that the information which are needed have already exist. In this case the most important aspect is to find efficient solution to access to this data and easy distribute it where it was requested. The Intranet is used similar to the Internet but it is private and secure which is very important for fragile data which organizations are using. Moreover Intranet is cost effective and allows limitless communication across geographical boundaries. In case of university the idea of Intranet can be used not only for the students but also for the teachers and administration employees which gives possibility to share the knowledge in very quick way but also additional information like grades, schedules or administrative changes.

- Project Management

Project management tools afford for high level of university to actions which are connected with creation of knowledge. This tools provide users to trace back artifacts and documents which might have caused from previous project. Despite of the project management tools meaning in creation of knowledge in organization is partial, this instruments can offer good foundation for storing and organizing all documents used in organization. In addition project management tools give possibility to connect used resources to the project management document, create reports or trace referenced hyperlinks. Thanks to this solution universities can exchange the best practice also between each other [9].

5 Knowledge Management Benefits

The benefits of knowledge management relate to three levels: organizations, employees and to the market.

1. Organizations level. For the organization, the benefits of knowledge management are established on two levels: inside of the organization and the outside of the organization (environment).

   The benefits of knowledge management inside of the organization include [10]:

   (a) increase of management efficiency: organizational culture allowing easy access to knowledge assets, building a new strategy, free flow of knowledge, increased importance of research, exchange of the best experiences, change in relations with clients and market partners, easy access to experts, dynamic development of information technology in the organization;
   (b) employee development: knowledge sharing among employees, employee systems motivation, systems staff development (increase in key competences), coaching, mentoring, team working (higher work efficiency);
   (c) improvements in communication inside of the organization: internal procedures establishing the principles of acquiring, processing and implementing knowledge (information), implementation of information technology.
   (d) reduction of management costs: by saving time, codification of knowledge, quick access to knowledge assets;
   (e) improve of creativity and innovation: exchange of knowledge and experience, focusing in employee development, building communities of practitioners and task teams;
   (f) increase in the flexibility of organization management: quick response on the environment information, constant monitoring of the market situation.

   The flow benefits of the external organizational level is about defense and development of the market position and increase in competitiveness through:

   (a) enterprise development: creating new values, continuous improving all aspects and at all levels of the organization;

(b) increase in the competitiveness of employees and enterprises: continuous employee education and qualifications, effective use of the employees potential;

(c) increase in the efficiency of action: limiting management costs, improvements in human resource management

(d) flexibility in adapting to the market needs: predicting client's and market partner's needs, as well as competition moves;

(e) innovation: creating new products and improving quality of products and services

(f) changes in customer relations: shaping a positive image of the company.

2. Employee level. The benefits of knowledge management apply not only to the organization but also to the employees. Creating an organizational culture cause free flow of the knowledge and leads employees development.

The benefits of knowledge management at the employee level are [11]:

(a) continuous development,

(b) improving competences,

(c) easy access to knowledge resources: better work performance and higher effectiveness,

(d) saving time: necessary to gain proper data,

(e) creativity: generating new values for the organization,

(f) self-realization,

(g) positive attitude to the work.

3. Market level. The benefits of knowledge management in context of market include both market partners – suppliers and customers as well as competitors. Such cooperation brings following benefits:

(a) fluent exchange of information, knowledge and experiences: in context of different organizations and cultures,

(b) understanding customer needs: new ideas for products and services,

(c) media effect: the company prestige increases and causes valuable business contacts,

(d) constant control of market changes: useful in preparing organization strategy.

The main result of all benefits is to shape efficient management system which consist new organizational strategy and organizational culture based on knowledge management and support by the information technologies.

6 Conclusions

Certainly new technologies will motivate institution connected with education to analysis and consideration about the entire process of learning and teaching. It gives possibility to simplify learning chances for individuals. Definitely it is still much work to do in field of modern education and the possibilities of development are very broad.

The main findings of the papers can be formulated as follows:

(1) Modern education needs to be systematically changed in order to react on actual challenges like modifying universities in the institution which are oriented more on the market by implementing new technologies, deploy new trends, follow and react on student expectations.

(2) There is a bigger and bigger importance of information technology in modern education. One of the most popular method which universities are using on their portals is e-learning which gives completely new possibilities of learning more focused on individual needs and skills of the users. Moreover this method can quickly measure the progress and possibility to establish proper program of learning.

(3) Universities and other educational institutions are obliged to apply knowledge management tools in didactics as well in other areas of their activities. In addition universities are using also tools which are useful in the administration like document management, project management or intranet. It improves the work of employees and provides continuous access to current information for the students Certainly this is the added value that enhances the competitive advantage.

The future research about developing and using new methods, tools and approaches in field of education will definitely focus more on effectiveness especially in context of individual needs of students but also in hybridization of the most efficient methods. Universities noticed that Knowledge Management is the key element which may generate measurable results in quality of teaching and organizing work. Such conditions favor the perception of the institution as an attractive place to develop its skills and knowledge which is so important in context of institution like university.

Undoubtedly the basic objective of Knowledge Management is extending the innovation capacity of organizations by better use of knowledge, talents or opportunities and technologies. Obviously it is not easy to apply KM mainly because it needs certain change of attitude, like listening instead of push, collaborating not competing, gathering, sharing experiences and evaluating the benefits [10].

References

1. Oprea, M.: A university knowledge management tool for academic research activity evaluation. Informatica Economică 15(3), 58 (2011)
2. Becerra-Fernandez, I.: Rajiv Sabherwal, Knowledge management: Systems and Processes. Routledge, New York (2015)
3. Mikuła, B., Pietruszka-Ortyl, A., Potocki, A.: Zarządzanie przedsiębiorstwem XXI wieku. Wybrane koncepcje i metody, Difin, Warszawa (2002)
4. Strojny, M.: Teoria i praktyka zarządzania wiedzą, Ekonomika i Organizacja Przedsiębiorstwa (2000)
5. https://beyond2015.acu.ac.uk/submissions/view?id=106
6. Marciniak, K., Owoc, M.L.: Knowledge management as foundation of smart university. Ganzha, M., Maciaszek, L.A., Paprzycki, M (eds.) Federated Conference on Computer Science and Information Systems - FedCSIS 2013, Kraków, Poland, 8–11 September 2013, Proceedings (2013)

7. Jones, G., Sallis, E.: Knowledge Management in Education: Enhancing Learning & Education. Routledge, Abingdon (2002)
8. Liebowitz, J., Frank, M.: Knowledge Management and E-Learning. CRC Press, Boca Raton (2010)
9. Arkorful, V., Abaidoo, N.: The role of e-learning, advantages and disadvantages of its adoption in higher education. Int. J. Instr. Technol. Distance Learn. **12**(1), 29–42 (2015)
10. Błaszczuk, A., Brdulak, J.J., Guzik, M., Pawluczuk, A.: Zarządzanie wiedzą w polskich przedsiębiorstwach, Szkoła Główna Handlowa, Warszawa (2004)
11. Kwiecień, K., Majewski, M.: Tajniki wykorzystania wiedzy, w: Zarządzanie wiedzą w przedsiębiorstwie, Materiały konferencyjne, Polska Fundacja Promocji Kadr, Warszawa (2001)
12. Mercier-Laurent, E.: Knowledge Management & Risk Management, Federal Conference on Computer Science and Information Systems (2016)
13. A Tiwana Knowledge Management Toolkit, Prentice Hall PTR (2002)

The Role of Knowledge Management in IT Projects

Piotr Domagała[✉]

Wroclaw University of Economics, Komandorska 118/120,
53-345 Wroclaw, Poland
piotr.domagala@ue.wroc.pl

Abstract. Project Management is a field of management dealing with using available knowledge, skills, tools and technology to fill needs and expectations of projects principles. The main goal of this article is to show how knowledge management powered by AI can be used in projects, why it is so important nowadays and how it can impact on the projects effectiveness in a positive way. In the first part of the paper the author focuses on definition and division of knowledge. The second part relates to project management basics. The last one focuses on role of knowledge management in projects.

Keywords: Knowledge · Knowledge management · Knowledge modeling · Project · Project management · IT project

1 Introduction

Project management is used in almost every field of human activity, ranging from military and space projects, through the wide range of typical design areas such as IT business, consulting, architecture, government programs and projects to new areas of PM such as pharmaceutical industry and health care.

This area especially derive from knowledge management to improve effectiveness of implemented projects. It is caused by increasing environment turbulence (law changes, new technologies development) and by the fact that unique knowledge which creates new products and services is an important source of the competitive advantage. This pressure has forced the organizations to bring innovation processes on improving performance and, by this way, to begin continuous learning and improving organizational processes.

According to the much research and surveys conducted by institutions of European Union which are responsible for supporting projects and programs, the crucial problem of realizing projects is inappropriate way of project knowledge managing, especially loss of organizational memory because of an insufficient ability to collect the project knowledge. It causes low effectiveness, poor results quality, dissatisfaction of commissioners and ineffective way of financial sources managing. Low level of learning and using experience, leads to aversion to implementation of new projects and loosing, as a consequence, opportunities from business point of view.

As a solution, more and more scientists and managers head towards the knowledge management. Knowledge management is a source of methodology and tools helpful to

© IFIP International Federation for Information Processing 2019
Published by Springer Nature Switzerland AG 2019
E. Mercier-Laurent and D. Boulanger (Eds.): AI4KM 2017, IFIP AICT 571, pp. 40–51, 2019.
https://doi.org/10.1007/978-3-030-29904-0_4

recognize, to get, to use and to collect knowledge which is necessary to realize complicated projects in better and more efficient way. Knowledge gathered during previous projects ensure better start for next ones. Managers can easily extract basic information about similar projects, predict possible problems, plan solutions to avoid them before begging of a project and make more reliable decisions based on previous experiences in the middle of a project which makes whole process more effective and less time-consuming. As a result, project knowledge management, the new area of science has been appearing before our eyes.

This field of knowledge, utilizes the existing, very rich heritage of knowledge management in the area of organizational management – the management of repetitive activities, based on permanent organizational structures and transfer it into the field of realization of complex, unique and time-limited projects.

2 Definition of Knowledge. Knowledge Management and Modeling

The knowledge that accompanies us in many situations and what has already been shown, is an indispensable part of the business. The first thing which should be explained is the definition of knowledge.

The term is traditionally considered as a triangle data-information-knowledge and it is illustrated as a pyramid (Fig. 1).

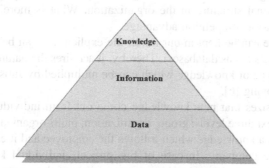

Fig. 1. Hierarchy of knowledge. Traditional approach. (Source: Own work based on Kowalczyk A., Nogalski B. (2007), p. 22. Diffin, Warszawa)

In spite of alternative shots, this model is accepted as the most appropriate in knowledge management. Attempts to create superior concepts in relation to knowledge, such as wisdom, have not been recognized as they meaning for philosophy rather than scientific and practical management challenges [1].

Misunderstanding of the differences between data, information and knowledge concepts can lead to inappropriate understanding of tools or misleading expectations e.g. misleading knowledge planning with information-planning systems.

The term of data can be understood as one sign or group of signs, arranged in accordance with the rules of a given syntax [2]. From technical point of view data can be recognized as set of cold facts and numbers without any context what prevents the use of data in its pure form [3].

Information is a narrower concept than data because it includes facts and figures that are presented in a comprehensible form to the recipient and do not duplicate the resources of current knowledge. Information can be defined as interpreted data, placed in a certain context [4]. It is necessary to point out that significant meaning from organizational point of view has only information which is helpful in whole management process and it is called as business information.

The term of knowledge is the most difficult to explain. Knowledge refers to the practical use of the information we have already acquired for a specific purpose. In many definitions we can find out that this term is used in relation to the problem solving.

The most popular classification of knowledge mark out explicite and tacit knowledge. The first one can be easily encoded or written in form of text and exchanged [5]. The essence of tacit knowledge can be easily illustrated by the example: We know someone's face and we are able to recognize it in the crowd, between thousands or billions other faces, but we cannot explain how we can do that. To be more specific – it cannot be expressed by words. This type of knowledge based on intuition, feelings, faith, life experiences and organizational culture. Explicite knowledge is important because of ability of collecting, sending and even selling. Tacit knowledge is especially important for the organization. It has the biggest impact on tasks implementation and efficiency of functional structure in the organization. What is more, it has also fundamental meaning as a competition advantage.

Tacit knowledge can be kept in our mind, the explicit one can be stored in written form (also electronic such as databases). Thereby, it acquires the nature of the available good and it is the type of knowledge which can be multiplied by subsequent processes of recording or copying [6].

Nonaka emphasizes that new knowledge come out from individual and then it is transferred to the next three levels: group, organization, multi-organization. The essence can be explained as a knowledge which follows the employee and it can be risky when someone leaves the company. In case of big projects individual knowledge is not enough and success depends on combining knowledge of the group (synergy effect). Organizational knowledge is interpreted as a total knowledge resources held by the organization. On the highest multi-organizational level occurs knowledge exchange [7].

Organizational learning is based on an organizational culture that promotes free communication and knowledge sharing between members of the organization. The basis for the smooth functioning of the learning organization is a strong and coherent vision of the organization, which must be communicated to all employees and implemented by them to promote strategic thinking as well as a strategy which is not only impassive, but also unequivocal [8]. An organization can be called learning if it can draw conclusions from its own past and build on it the routine practices that underpin its behavior [9].

Knowledge management is a relatively new interdisciplinary business model that covers the fields of economic sciences, management, information technology, telematics, sociology, linguistics, and psychology. It combines strategies, tools and techniques that are often known and used for many years [10]. Almost all of the definitions have a few common points that identify knowledge management in the most precise way [11]:

- using of external sources,
- collecting knowledge resources in business processes, products and services,
- representing knowledge in databases and documents,
- promoting the growth of knowledge resources through the development of organizational culture and motivation,
- transferring and sharing knowledge across the organization,
- regular assessment of the value and impact of knowledge assets.

Based on knowledge diversification proposed by Polanyi, we can identify knowledge management as a set of processes that transform the knowledge of the workers and tacit knowledge from the organizational environment into the valuable resources of the knowledge that makes it possible to gain competitive advantage.

Knowledge management as a complex process that depends on the character of the organization, requires a well-thought out strategy and assumes certain priorities. Two most popular strategies developed by M.T. Hansen and T. Tierney are [12]:

- codification strategy, based on explicit knowledge that involves collecting and sharing knowledge in the computer databases,
- personalization strategy, based on tacit knowledge that giving opportunity for sharing knowledge between employees, computer systems are not as useful as they are in the codification strategy.

As it was mentioned above, knowledge can take a shape hard to describe and codify. Surprisingly, there are tools which can be helpful in resolving this problem. Knowledge modeling is a cross disciplinary approach to capture and model knowledge into a reusable format for purpose of preserving, improving, sharing, substituting, aggregating and reapplying it. In the computer world it is used to simulate intelligence. Innovation, progress and prosperity, all depends heavily on making the right decisions. The good news is that making right decisions is not hard. For a rational agent there is no way of making wrong decisions, given "all" the facts and a "clear" objective. The only reason for making wrong decisions is by neglecting the facts or misinterpreting the goal. That is why knowledge modeling is such a critical element of cognitive discipline and a prerequisite for reaching true Artificial Intelligence. knowledge modeling offers a shift from local proprietary solutions to produce and disseminate embedded Knowledge Models into larger computational solutions in effort to generate "applied knowledge." It contributes to scores of intellectual activities, from continuous improvement to automated decision-making or problem-solving, and hence increases "Intellectual Capital" for generations of humankind to come. The fundamental goal of knowledge modeling is to bring methodologies and technologies together in an implementation neutral framework as a practical solution for maximizing the leverage of knowledge. The core difference between working with information and knowledge is that - in addition to facts - a knowledge model includes enactment and has the ability to support intuition as well as the subjectivity of experts and/or users. In everyday situations, people make a variety of decisions to act upon. In turn, these decisions vary based on one's preferences, objectives and habits. The following example, Fig. 2 – Situational Effects, highlights how gender and age play a role in the decision-making process.

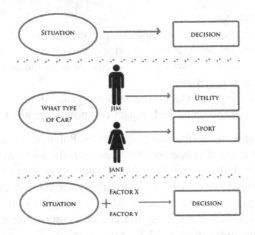

Fig. 2. Situational effects (Source: Own work based on Makhfi Pejman, Introduction to Knowledge Modeling, www.makhfi.com/KCM_intro.htm [31.07.2017])

As such, many models, like the example of Jim and Jane, can only be executed after having a profile assigned. A profile is defined as the personnel interpretation of inputs to a model. knowledge modeling incorporate the quantitative and qualitative use of information, and processes tangible and intangible attributes that contribute to end result, such as Jim's decision of buy a sport's car. The bridging together of quantitative and qualitative methods enables knowledge modeling to incorporate subjectivity, which is the main differentiator between information and knowledge. Knowledge models help us to learn from past decisions, to assess present activities and, just as important, to preserve domain expertise. Knowledge saves time and overhead costs, and reduces the mistakes from overlooks. Knowledge models are very valuable and often outlive a particular implementation and/or project. Accordingly, the challenge of knowledge modeling is that this process must be designed not only as an abstract idea, but as an implementable process with the ability to aggregate and disseminate applied knowledge for the purpose of creating intellectual capital for generations of humankind to come. As a best practice approach knowledge models should stay implementation neutral and provide experts with flexibility of picking the appropriate technology for each specific implementation. In general the technology solutions can be categorized into case-based systems and knowledge-based systems. Case-based approach focuses on solving new problems by adapting previously successful solutions to similar problems and focuses on gathering knowledge from case histories. To solve a current problem: the problem is matched against similar historical cases and adjusted accordingly to specific attributes of new case. As such they don't require an explicit knowledge elicitation from experts. Expert or knowledge based systems (KBS) on the other hand focuses on direct knowledge elicitation from experts. There are a variety of methods and technologies that can be utilized in knowledge modeling, including some practices with overlapping features. The most commonly used methods are highlighted below [13] (Table 1):

Tabel 1. Knowledge modeling methods (Source: Own work based on Makhfi Pejman, Introduction to Knowledge Modeling, www.makhfi.com/KCM_intro.htm [31.07.2017])

Decision tree & AHP	Graph of options and their possible consequences used to create a plan in order to reach a common goal. This approach provides designers with a structured model for capturing and modeling knowledge appropriate to a concrete-type application
	Closely related to a decision tree, AHP (Analytic Hierarchy Process) developed by Dr. Thomas Saaty bestows a powerful approach to Knowledge Modeling by incorporating both qualitative and quantitative analysis
Bayesian networks & ANP	Influence-based systems such as Bayesian Network (Belief Network) or ANP (Analytic Network Process) provide an intuitive way to identify and embody the essential elements, such as decisions, uncertainties, and objectives in effort to better understand how each one influence the other
Artificial neural network	An Artificial Neural Network (ANN) is a non-linear mathematical or computational model for information processing. In most cases, ANN is an adaptive system that changes its structure based on external or internal information that flows through the network. It also addresses issues by adapting previously successful solutions to similar problems
Genetic & evolutionary algorithms	Inspired by biological evolution, including inheritance, mutation, natural selection, and recombination (or crossover), genetic and evolutionary algorithms are used to discover approximate solutions that involve optimization and problem searching in explorative models (refer to model types)
Expert systems	Expert systems are the forefathers of capturing and reusing experts' knowledge, and they typically consist of a set of rules that analyze information about a specific case. Expert systems also provide an analysis of the problem(s). Depending upon its design, this type of system will produce a result, such as recommending a course of action for the user to implement the necessary corrections
Statistical models	Statistical models are mathematical models developed through the use of empirical data. Included within this group are (1) simple and/or multiple linear regression, (2) variance-covariance analysis, and (3) mixed models

(continued)

Tabel 1. (*continued*)

Rule engines	Another effective tool for knowledge modeling is a rule engine, which is categorized as an inference rule engine or a reactive rule engines
	The inference rule engines is used to answer complex questions in order to infer possible answers. For example, a Mortgage Company would ask – "Should this customer be allowed a loan to buy a house?"
	Reactive rule engines are used to detect and react to interesting patterns of events occurring and reacting
Workflow systems	A Workflow System manages the operational aspect of a work procedure, analyzing (1) how tasks are structured, (2) who performs them, (3) what their relative order is, (4) how they are synchronized, (5) how information flows to support the tasks, and (6) how tasks are being tracked. Workflow problems can be modeled and analyzed using graph-based formalisms like Petri nets

As we can see in the table above, there are a lot of possible solutions to use knowledge management methods powered by artificial intelligence. There are also plenty of benefits which should encourage to use them. All of them enable to reduce decision-making process in time, improve the productivity of process and staff, reduce costs, automate our actions, reduce risk of making mistakes. These are only examples of tangible benefits. It is worth to point out a few intangible advantages such as: positive influence on organizational transparency and reliability, accurateness and faster access to data for timely decisions, saving enormous time and effort in data entry, facilitates strategic planning etc.

Interpretation of knowledge and knowledge management is not a simple task. It depends on many aspects and point of view. Researchers and business practitioners try to define it as precisely as possible but it seems to be unenforceable because of dynamic changes in the environment. We can only approximate general characteristics. Artificial intelligence tools give us opportunity to improve decision making process and find solutions very quickly which is desirable in managing projects. In the next part of the paper the author will present how areas of knowledge management and projects interpermeate each other.

3   Knowledge Management in Projects

Due to the rapidly growing popularity of projects in recent years, acknowledged by someone as even the fashion of management, it is necessary to clearly delineate their conceptual boundaries.

Project Management Institute, the biggest organization gathering project managers, treats projects as "A temporary action undertaken to create a unique product or service" [14]. As a temporality we should understand time constraint of project "life" (defined time of project beginning and end) and it do not need to be recognized absolutely as a short time of realization. According to PMI definition, the aim of the project can be understood as delivering specific, unique result, product or service. Specific because of requirements, scope, circumstances, suppliers and other characteristics.

Why project management is so popular today? Companies are increasingly implementing their operations at the operational and strategic level in the form of projects. Projects are helpful in reconstructing and rebuilding agency assets by raising the value of the organization for its stakeholders [15]. Project management is used in almost all fields of business, starting with space and military projects through popular areas such as IT, consulting and architecture to new areas of music business, movies, health care and pharmaceutical business [16].

We can consider three main parameters (constraints):

- result quality and fulfill requirements,
- time and deadline,
- costs.

Parameters mentioned above are classified as elements conditioning project success. A lot of scientist treat as an insufficient and create additional ones e.g. client satisfaction, keeping current organizational culture etc. [17].

The specificity of knowledge management in projects and the uniqueness of the issues within this scope is directly rooted in the definition and characteristics of projects [18]. We can divide organizations activity according to repeatability and complexity criteria into four groups: routine activities (high repeatability and low complexity), functions (high repeatability and complexity), improvised activities (low repeatability and rather low complexity) and projects (low repeatability and rather high or high complexity) [19] (Fig. 3).

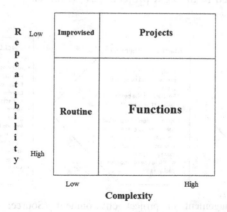

Fig. 3. Kind of activities in organizations. (Source: Own work based on 19. Trocki M., Grucza B., Ogonek K. (2003), p. 14. Zarządzanie Wiedzą, PWE.)

Typical and traditional area of interest for knowledge management are functions - complex and traditional action/processes. Because of its complexity, realization is strongly connected with collecting and processing of significant knowledge sources.

Their repeatability let relatively easy record. What is more, repeatability make the new sets of knowledge easy to obtain and update according to the Deming cycle. Projects are complex and require (similar to functions) big sources of knowledge. In contrast to functions, projects are not repeatable and, as a consequence, projects are unaffiliated to stiff regulations. Due to this fact, they are very often compared to the art of project management [20].

The project uniqueness causes a lot of questions about the knowledge uniqueness used in projects. Can knowledge used in one project, be useful in the other projects? Can we consider knowledge from previous projects (lessons learned) as a valuable source of the knowledge for the organization? We can bring it to the level of project knowledge specificity and to the level of mobility. The crucial aspect of creating an individual knowledge management system in the organization is to keep balance between general sources of knowledge and specific project experiences connected to the project in a particular environment.

Another challenge for knowledge management in projects is to deliver appropriate knowledge in appropriate time. It is related to two appearances. First of all, people who start working in the project, should have sufficient knowledge at the beginning. In the other case, the knowledge should be delivered as soon as possible and according to all needs. For example, project manager who has been chosen from the team without any experience in management and procedure awareness in the organization, should be involved in intense training. Secondly, every step in the project is related with specific problems and specific set of knowledge which is needed to solve them. Especially important from knowledge management point of view is closing the project because it is connected with dissolution of a project team. Ignoring the stage of project closure in knowledge management processes can cause distraction and even significant loss of project knowledge. The main challenge at this stage is to keep the knowledge after project and let it be used in the next projects [21] (Fig. 4).

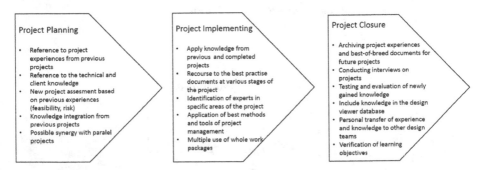

Fig. 4. Knowledge management in project environment (Source: Own work based on Hanisch B., Lindner F., Mueller A., Wald A., Knowledge management in project environments. Journal of Knowledge Management, 2009, 13 (4), p. 150.)

More examples of knowledge management through project management stages are presented at the diagram above.

The teamwork nature of the project strongly influences on the specificity of knowledge management. At first, knowledge and specialized skills should be treated as a main criteria of selecting staff for the project team. As it was mentioned before, we should not loss time and resources for trainings and other methods of learning at the beginning of the project. There is a strong need for employee information and their qualifications in the early phases of the project. This information should be collected and stored independently of ongoing projects, to let managers use it in every moment during the project. Another challenge is to ensure high level of communication between team members because of their functional and knowledge diversification. Hermetic language, specified vocabulary, conviction about the superiority of own expertise knowledge inhibit the knowledge management processes and also cooperation. The third aspect of teamwork nature is project teams autonomy. Autonomy very often stunts learning process in organization [22]. Inadequate control and project coordination can lead to knowledge retention in individual projects, unwillingness to share it outside the team, loss of knowledge, and even the use of individual practices and tools that are not in line with organizational standards and policies [23].

By analyzing internal environment we cannot forget about tacit knowledge. According to the studies, people are almost five times more eager to look for information in their closest environment. They prefer to ask friends rather than search for the answer in the database or documents. The most common way to reach knowledge will be through informal activities, based on friends networks, such us sending e-mail, short informal calls or meetings. The knowledge gathered by each employee will be determine by the position in the company or role in the project. It causes the risk of reluctance to share it with the others. In the reference to personalization strategy is better to lead moderate expenses on IT and let put people in contact with colleagues [24]. It is the phenomenon strictly corresponding with the process of knowledge externalization. Gathering knowledge derived directly from individuals is possible only on the condition that they want to share it with the others. It is a difficult task for managers to create friendly atmosphere and organizational culture conducive to knowledge share but it is also one of the keys to projects succeed [7].

4 Summary

The specific features of the projects detailed and discussed in this paper have a very strong influence on the specificity and priorities of knowledge management in projects. Summarizing, let introduce the following conclusions:

- project implementation requires advanced interdisciplinary knowledge (with a view to the complexity of project innovation),
- project knowledge is dispersed (due to the task and temporary character of the project team),
- this knowledge must be described at an appropriate level of detail to ensure its transferability between projects,
- the basic object of the project management knowledge management process should be the project team,
- technical (object-oriented) knowledge is an essential element of project knowledge.

The use of knowledge management methods in project implementation is an object of interest for researchers from knowledge management and professionals dealing with complex and unique projects. They focus especially on impact of KM according to three main project success parameters, pointed out in the third paragraph of the section "Knowledge management in projects" because it give us the answer on the question how it is used in projects nowadays and what we can do to develop its usability in the future. The author tries to refine them by describing specific benefits in the Table 2.

Tabel 2. Overall and specific benefits cause of knowledge management in projects (Source: own work based on Schwaab J., Knowledge management for project managers and other decision-makers – Learning from experience. Deutsche Gesellschaft fur Technische Zusammenarbeit, Eschborn, 2009, p. 2)

Advantages	Specific benefits for project teams
Cost reduction	- Study on own mistakes and mistakes committed in other projects - Quick and easy training of employees - Use good practices and existing solutions - Avoid duplication of work
Time saving	- Sharing experience and team communication without conflicts - Avoid duplication of work and wasting time - Use of ideas from other design teams
Quality improving	- Improving the quality of results through a good design concept - Competent partnerships - Good local coordination with the other project participants - Experience-based learning with a business partner - Common direction of the teams

Particular interest is given to the benefits that the project can achieve in the case of adequate management of knowledge resources.

Introduction to knowledge management solutions in the area of project management can significantly improve the efficiency and effectiveness of process execution. However, these solutions should be based on justified grounds.

References

1. Jashapara, A.: Knowledge Management, pp. 34–35. FT Prentice Hall, Harlow (2004)
2. Probst, G., Raub, S., Romhardt, K.: Zarządzanie wiedzą w organizacji, p. 21. Oficyna Ekonomiczna, Cracow (2004)
3. Jashapara, A.: Knowledge Management, p. 32. FT Prentice Hall, Harlow (2004)
4. Floridi, L.: Is information meaningful data? Philos. Phenomenol. Res. **70**(2), 351–370 (2005)
5. Tiwana, A.: The Knowledge Management Toolkit: Orchestrating IT, Strategy and Knowledge Platform, pp. 57–59. Prentice Hall PTR, Harlow (2002)
6. Polanyi, M. foreword by Sen A.: The Tacit Dimension, p. 50. The University of Chicago Press, Chicago (2009)

7. Nonaka, I.: A dynamic theory of organizational knowledge creation. Organ. Sci. **5**(1), 14–37 (1994)
8. Armstrong, M., Taylor, S.: Armstrong's Handbook of Human Resources Management Practice, 13th edn, pp. 284–287 (2014)
9. Garwin, D.A.: Building Learning Organization. Business Harvard Review, July–August 1993
10. Dalkir, K.: Knowledge Management in Theory and Practice, pp. 21–24. Elsevier Butterworth–Heinemann (2005)
11. Awad, E.M., Ghaziri, H.M.: Knowledge Management, pp. 26–27. Pearson Education, New Jersey (2004)
12. Hansen, M.T., Nohira, N., Tierney, T.: What's your strategy for managing knowledge? Harvard Bus. Rev. **77**(2), 106–116 (1999)
13. http://www.makhfi.com/KCM_intro.htm. Accessed 31 July 2017
14. PMI: Guide to Project Management Body of Knowledge, 4th edn, pp. 5–6. Project Management Institute Inc. (2008)
15. Nokes, S., Kelly, S.: The Definitive Guide to Project Management, p. 89. Prentice Hall (2007)
16. Semadeni, M., Anderson, B.: The follower's dilemma: innovation and imitation in the professional services industry. Acad. Manag. J. **53**(5), 1175–1193 (2010)
17. Kerzer, H.: Project Management, A Systems Approach to Planning, Scheduling and Controlling, 8th edn, p. 6. Wiley (2003)
18. Canonico, P., Soderlund, J., De Nito, E., Mangia, G.: Special issue on organizational mechanism for effective knowledge creation in projects: guest editorial. Int. J. Manag. Projects Bus. **6**(2), 223–235 (2013)
19. Trocki, M., Grucza, B., Ogonek, K.: Zarządzanie Wiedzą, p. 14. PWE, Warszawa (2003)
20. Berkun, S.: The Art of Project Management. O'Reilly Media Inc. (2005)
21. Brady, T., Davies, A.: Building project capabilities: from exploratory to exploitative learning. Organ. Stud. **25**(9), 1601–1621 (2004)
22. Hobday, M.: The project-based organization: an ideal form for managing complex products and systems? Res. Policy **29**(7–8), 871–893 (2000)
23. Scarbrough, H., Swan, J., Laurent, S., Bresen, M.: Project-based learning and the role of learning boundaries. Organ. Stud. **25**(9), 1579–1600 (2004)
24. Allen, T.: Managing the Flow of Technology. MIT Press, Cambridge (1977)

Dynamical Aspects of Knowledge Evolution

Tracking Changes in Knowledge Bases

Mieczysław Owoc[1(✉)] and Paweł Weichbroth[2]

[1] Wroclaw University of Economics, ul. Komandorska 118/120,
Wrocław, Poland
mieczyslaw.owoc@ue.wroc.pl
[2] WSB University in Gdansk, ul. Grunwaldzka 238A, 80-266 Gdańsk, Poland
pweichbroth@wsb.gda.pl

Abstract. Undeniably, in this rapidly changing world some knowledge granules change over time. Tracking these changes seems to be one of the most crucial processes in knowledge management. Every potential change is a result of knowledge adoption and application to solve a given problem or task in particular domains. However, there is a lack of a model that provides an event-driven framework, along with the core adoption process explicitly expressed with related factors, which together serve as an efficient tool to adopt and reuse knowledge on one hand, while on the other, to measure and evaluate the various aspects of knowledge quality and usefulness. This paper aims to fill this gap by introducing a knowledge adoption process and an ontology-aided encapsulation knowledge (OAKE) model. While the former breaks down the tacit adoption process into two explicit sub-processes and measurable factors, the latter exposes knowledge evolution over time by a sequence of recorded events.

Keywords: Knowledge · Dynamics · Evolution · Adoption · Management

1 Introduction

"Tacit, complex knowledge, developed and internalized by the knower over a long period of time, is almost impossible to reproduce in a document or database. Such knowledge incorporates so much accrued and embedded learning that its rules may be impossible to separate from how an individual acts" [1].

Moreover, considering the issue of knowledge reproduction, one could ask: how does knowledge change over time, and what are the origins and reasons of the occurring changes? Similarly, advanced-in-age knowledge has accumulated so many changes as a result of the cognition of its nature and has been so enriched by learning that its evolution may be impossible to reconstruct.

Knowledge is a wide and abstract term, which has been the subject of an epistemological discussion of western philosophers since times of ancient Greece. Since the second half of XX century, knowledge has been widely studied in numerous research papers, uncovering many definitions, contexts and phenomena and in the end leading to a legitimate new scientific discipline, defined as knowledge management [2–4]. For an

© IFIP International Federation for Information Processing 2019
Published by Springer Nature Switzerland AG 2019
E. Mercier-Laurent and D. Boulanger (Eds.): AI4KM 2017, IFIP AICT 571, pp. 52–65, 2019.
https://doi.org/10.1007/978-3-030-29904-0_5

organization, knowledge has become the most powerful leverage to achieve a competitive advantage, therefore it is crucial to effectively manage own resources [5–7].

These days, people and machines produce countless volumes of data and information, consciously and intentionally transformed into knowledge. All of the aforementioned are important assets in knowledge-driven environments and the last is by far the most labour- and time-consuming [8–10]. In consequence, some employees spend the majority of their working hours doing manual, high-demanding intellectual work, supported by computers processing and manipulating large amounts of data as an input, and producing information or even knowledge as an output [11–13]. As a result, a new concept of an employee was coined: "a knowledge worker", whose job primarily involves the creation, distribution and application of knowledge [14]. By many, Peter Drucker is credited to be the first to use this term in his 1959 book, "Landmarks of Tomorrow" [15, 16].

Data sets encoded in a computer memory differ in format, size and type. In general use, there are two primary data formats: binary and text, and four primary data types: text, drawing, movie and voice. Ordered sequences of characters, images and spoken words are perceived as explicit and unique information objects. Here, we can point out objects that are in everyday use, such as documents, presentations and spreadsheets, email-, voice- and video- messages, and web- blogs, forums and pages. Each object processed and interpreted by an individual human mind, applicable and legitimate in a specified environment, where the consequences of the application are known or can be predicted, is considered to be a knowledge object. All of these objects, gathered and redacted, cleaned and re-processed, organized and integrated in one consistent repository, along with a user interface that facilitates SCRUD operations (an acronym for search, create, read and delete), constitute a unified platform for knowledge workers.

However, knowledge workers are still looking for a comprehensive solution to manage knowledge in such a manner that it will not only serve as pure technology but also provide interaction with other humans and available resources [17–19]. At present, in the development of knowledge management (KM), to the best of our knowledge, there is a lack of a consensual framework, or generic process model, for tracking knowledge evolution; instead, to some extent, each organization follows its own set of principles, design criteria and practices in this area. Most existing frameworks and tools broadly touch the area of KM, and only a few are targeted specifically at tracking knowledge evolution. This paper aims to fill this gap by proposing an ontology-aided knowledge encapsulation (OAKE) model, along with a knowledge cognition model.

The rest of the paper is organized as follows. The literature review is given in Sect. 2. In Sect. 3, at first, the knowledge cognition model is introduced followed by the OAKE model. Final conclusions are included in Sect. 4.

2 Literature Review

The recent interest in knowledge management (KM), observed both in business and science, is nothing new. Therefore, it is no secret that nowadays, information and communication technologies (ICT) are the basic means to efficiently support every phase of the KM process. However, diverse technologies, such as knowledge management systems, knowledge discovery systems and knowledge-based systems are currently working with different types of knowledge [20–22]. In our paper knowledge management is a term for any operations focused on knowledge granulas embracing all typical phases: discovering, registering, transformation and utilization. Another words, KM is a discipline that covers ideas and concepts from a variety of other disciplines, including artificial intelligence, data mining, distributed databases, information systems, intellectual capital and innovation [23–25].

Knowledge management is the process of continually managing knowledge of all kinds to meet existing and emerging needs, to identify and exploit existing and acquired knowledge assets and to develop new opportunities [26]. From a practical business perspective, it is a deliberate, systematic business optimization strategy that selects, distills, stores, organizes, packages, and communicates information essential to the business of a company in a manner that improves employee performance and corporate competitiveness [27]. In a narrow sense, it can be defined as a set of principles, processes, and techniques leading to the creation, organization, distribution, use and exploitation of knowledge [28, 29]. Crucial for the defined paper topic seems to be consideration of the phases directly connected with knowledge dynamics. In the next sections these selected KM operations will be discussed.

2.1 Knowledge Transformation

There are two basic forms of knowledge: tacit and explicit [30, 31]. The former refers to that which is unarticulated, undocumented and held in peoples' heads, while the latter is expressed, structured, codified and accessible for those other than the individuals originating it [32]. Thus, knowledge exists on the spectrum of these extremes and its transformation means moving from one extreme to another [33–35].

There are many reasons to engage means to perform knowledge transformation. The same or very similar problems do not need to be solved again – the particular pieces of knowledge can be reused. Effective reuse is apparently related to the effectiveness of the organization [36], and is an even more frequent concern when compared to knowledge creation, being viewed as somehow more important and difficult to manage [37]. In the theory of knowledge reusability, Markus [38] emphasizes the role of knowledge management systems and knowledge repositories, often called organizational memory systems, in the efficient preservation of "intellectual capital" [39–41]. Basically, knowledge transformation process can be identified with changing of existing knowledge or even with its creation applying for example process-driven approaches [42–44].

2.2 Knowledge Codification

The codification of knowledge is the process of converting knowledge into a form in which it can be handled by particular technology to store, transfer and share it [45]. In addition, it makes knowledge visible, accessible and usable in a form and a structure meaningful to the user [46]. Note, the knowledge code used during implementation (moving to a computer memory) is crucial to evaluate its usefulness and appropriateness. Coded knowledge should have a unique identity and an adequate form of representation, such as a rule, a decision table or tree, a model for problem solving and case-based reasoning or a knowledge map. To store and disseminate knowledge across an organization, various IT technologies, such as databases [47], intranets [48, 49] and business intelligence tools, are usually put into action [50–52]. In such a context the codification phase can be considered as the supporting operation of knowledge transformation but stressing its more technological nature [53–55].

2.3 Knowledge Adoption and Reuse

Knowledge adoption concerns an internalization phase of organizational knowledge transfer [56], in which explicit information is transformed into internalized knowledge and meaning [57]. In general, adoption usually begins with the recognition of the need for information, then moves to searching in possessed repositories, next to the initial decision to accept the received information, followed by validation in practice, and ending with absorption. On the other hand, knowledge provides the means to analyze and understand data and information [58–60], delivering the circumstances for an internal agreement between what we know and what we want to know.

The process of knowledge reuse consists of the following phases: capturing, packaging, distributing and reusing [38, 61]. In the human mind, the latter involves both recall and recognition, while the former concerns information attributes, such as: the author, the date of creation, the representation form, and eventually the storage location. Moreover, the latter tries to determine the relevance degree of the incoming information, and possibly append it to pending knowledge to be applied again [62].

Retained and reused knowledge can improve project management capabilities [63], support managers in the decision-making process [64–66] and guide the product design [67]. To be innovative and develop novel products and services, organizations need to gain knowledge of both external and internal worlds [68, 69]. To achieve these ends, the principal goal should be to focus on tracking changes occurring in internal bodies of knowledge.

3 Ontology-Aided Knowledge Encapsulation Model

All the mentioned knowledge phases are crucial in the created models supporting its dynamicity. In order to define a concept useful in modelling dynamical aspects of knowledge important assumptions should be declared. The name of the elaborated model comes from a conscious merger of the major concepts involved. Though the first term – ontology-aided may be unquestionable, while the term – encapsulation needs to tell a brief story. By definition, data and any appropriate operations should be grouped together i.e. encapsulated, and the implementation details of both should be hidden from the users [70]. A similar assumption was made in the elaborated model, where an operation is featured by an event. To implement the TBox part of the ontology, i.e. terminological knowledge declared as axioms and defined by a set of concepts and roles (the global axioms and core taxonomy), the Cognitum Ontorion system was used with the built-in capability of English semi-natural language support [55, 71].

This section begins with a description of the prior model, which provides the operational foundation for the later model.

3.1 The Knowledge Adoption Model

Knowledge adoption has been defined in many different ways. Beesley and Cooper [72] defined it as "identification of new products, services, markets, or processes", while Brown [73] as "the means through which policy-makers digest, accept then 'take on board' research finding". However, to the best of our knowledge, none of them does not reflect the general idea laying behind the nature of the process. Thus, for us, knowledge adoption means the acceptance of the state about the way things are and how they work, followed by the confirmation and judgment of its significance and value in the frame of present context and individual beliefs [31, 74].

These two actions we have previously defined as verification and evaluation – both included to more universal term: validation, respectively [12, 75]. For others, the former refers to reaching an agreement over the meaning of a term [76], involving concept matching and relation comparison [77, 78], while the latter refers to the evaluation of quality and usefulness [79, 80].

In terms of knowledge verification, three factors have been distinguished: adequacy, completeness and consistency [81]. The first factor corresponds to the degree of applicability or relevance to a given problem or task, the second refers to the degree to which the knowledge for completing a task or making a decision is passable and available, and the third refers to the degree of a logical match between the object and the content. In terms of knowledge evaluation, two factors have been identified: reliability and effectiveness. Both factors concern some kind of knowledge assessment, while the former reflects a degree of agreement to self-beliefs and experience, the latter refers to the outcomes of the applied knowledge (Fig. 1).

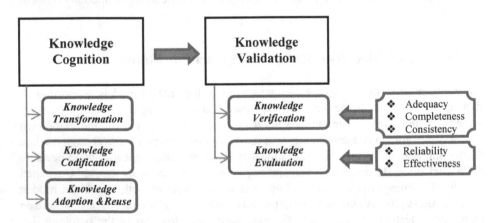

Fig. 1. The model of the knowledge adoption process (KAP)

These general factors can be expanded and elucidated in the form of interpretable numeric, logic or fuzzy metrics, to an extent appropriate to the context and the size of the knowledge object. If some errors, obstacles and constraints are observed, a need for change in a body of knowledge occurs.

3.2 The OAKE Model

The objective is neither to introduce a model which outlines all possible phases, tasks or relationships underlying the knowledge evolution process, nor to set up a strict list of guidelines to follow which positively affect organizational performance. Instead, the model highlights a few major factors that can expose the origins of and reasons for the occurred changes in particular bodies of knowledge over time (Fig. 2).

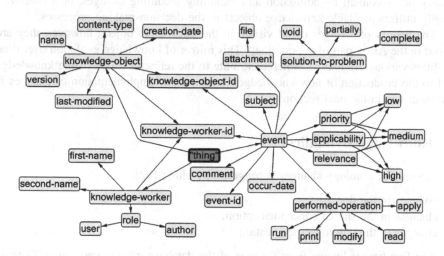

Fig. 2. The OAKE model

The aim of building the model is to capture changes in such a way that allows us to query and infer from the gathered knowledge. It is based on the observations collected from a requirements elicitation project for virtual on-line agents, where different groups of stakeholders, during the development of the knowledge base, reported heterogeneous requests to include itemized changes, often comparable or self-conflicting.

Each change is represented by a unique event, performed by a knowledge worker on the knowledge object. The notion of a single event is structured and formalized in the form of an ontology that provides a common understanding of performed operations and perceived observations.

Each single event object has a unique identifier and occurrence date, both automatically generated by the system. A knowledge worker inputs the subject that should generally reflect the idea laying beyond the event. Next, a type of performed operation on the knowledge object is selected, where a set of five options are available in multiple choice (apply, modify, read, run, print). The degree of priority, applicability and relevance are assigned, where each can be defined as low, medium or high. Next, a knowledge worker points to what degree (void, partially, complete) he found a solution to a problem or a task in the particular knowledge object and, if necessary, can also add a comment and attach a file. The event object is connected through two separate relations with the knowledge object and the knowledge worker.

The knowledge object has a name that, specified by a user, should reflect its content in general terms, as well as an accurate type in which the information is encoded for storage in a computer file. The creation date is a predefined property that corresponds to the date of the first version, while the last modified property shows the date where the last changes were made. A built-in mechanism provides unique version numbers for unique states of knowledge objects, assigned in increasing order to new developments.

The knowledge worker is identified by their first and second name and may play two different roles: an author (a creator) of the knowledge object, responsible for the quality of its content by admission and including incoming changes, or a user who simply utilizes available knowledge objects in the decision-making processes.

The history of changes is not visible in the knowledge object; however, they are stored in the ABox part of the ontology. This mirror of knowledge evolution over time facilities various evaluations which contribute to the refinement of existing knowledge and to the production of new knowledge. A concept of implementation of changes is demonstrated in the next section.

4   Knowledge Dynamics

The capture of ontology changes is triggered by either [82]:

- changes in the domain,
- changes in the shared conceptualization,
- changes in the ontology specification.

The first type is known from the area of the database schema versioning. Domain evolution, reflected and described by the changes, concern seven different facets [83]:

- heterogeneous instances: over time different occurrences of the same value have different meanings in a domain extension; for instance, if the organization merge or split departments, then the preserved naming represent a different set of resources (e.g. employees, faculties);
- cardinality changes: in particular, cardinality relationships between domains might also change over time; in other words, the number of occurrences in one entity which are associated to the number of occurrences in another are not always constant; for example, a *1-to-n* relationship between departments and faculties may be changed to *m-to-n* as a result of new legal regulations;
- granularity transition: from existing population values, having different granularity, might be added to a domain extension; for instance, the numeration of rooms or buildings might be changed due to the merge or acquisition [84, 85];
- encoding changes: particular values might have also encoded meaning, which neither is known, nor provided elsewhere; for example, the naming of projects successfully delivered are eventually different from the others (failed, cancelled, etc.; see [86]);

- time zone and unit differences: organization sites use local time zone and units which globally differ; thus directly comparing such values may be irrelevant;
- identifier changes: the organization needs changes over time; as a consequence the indexing strategies may also change over time, leading in parallel or overlapping naming schemas; for instance, the codes of the products, previously 4-digits numbers, now having additional 6 zeros, are different for both the users and IT systems;
- field recycling: in some systems it is difficult or even infeasible to alter certain database properties; in this case there might be a need to shrink the database or even implement a new instance with a different naming schema, replacing the existing ones; for example, a company might shift from hierarchical to a matrix structures, remodeling data structures [87–89].

The second type of the source of the ontology changes concern the assumption of the static nature of the shared conceptualization. Nowadays, it is at least naive to define specification in terms of the fixed settings, undeniably constant over time. On the contrary, many studies describe ontologies as dynamic networks of meaning [90–92].

Eventually, the third type is associated with ontology encoding, which may vary in types and formats. Along with ontology evolution, engineers are currently facing also the issue of merging ontologies [93–95].

In order to tracking of changes ontology presented in the OAKE model we reduce list of objects (Fig. 3).

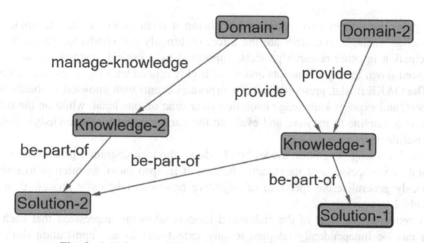

Fig. 3. Initial stage of the partially incorporated OAKE model

The most important objects are placed in the Figure; previously defined relationships are actual: Knowledge, Domains and Solutions. Assuming changes in the Domains the discussed ontology is presented in Fig. 4.

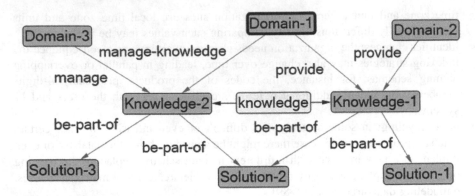

Fig. 4. Final stage of the partially incorporated OAKE model

List of the defined categories has been extended as a result of knowledge dynamics; next specimens appeared in case of Domains and Solutions and particular relationships mapped these new items. Comparing gradually appearing versions of ontology we are able to monitor knowledge dynamics supporting new solutions and taking into account new domains.

5 Conclusions

This paper introduces two models which bring a contribution to the discipline of knowledge management. Both are the effect of broadly self-conducted research and participation in other research projects, supported by a critical analysis of literature, narrowed down to major concepts and those highly related with the discussed subject.

The OAKE model, presented here, incorporates events with knowledge objects and workers, and exposes knowledge evolution over time on one hand, while on the other hand, is a baseline to measure and evaluate the various aspects of knowledge quality and usefulness.

The knowledge cognition model breaks down the tacit cognition process into two explicit sub-processes and measurable factors. It is, ipso facto, an attempt to unambiguously generalize the spectrum of cognitive processes inherently processed in an individual human mind.

A retrospective view of the elaborated models gives the impression that each of them can be independently adopted to any extent and in any application domain. However, both only embody general concepts with a high degree of abstraction, but not biased at any level, and can be further extended and attributed, eventually providing a framework to adopt and reuse knowledge with support for event-based tracking of changes.

References

1. Davenport, T.H., Prusak, L.: Working Knowledge: How Organizations Manage What They Know. Harvard Business Press, New York (1998)
2. Jakubczyc, J., Mercier-Laurent, E., Owoc, M.L.: What is knowledge management. In: Baborski, A. (ed.) Research Papers of Wrocław Economic Academy, no. 815 (1999)
3. Michalik, K.: Systemy ekspertowe we wspomaganiu procesów zarządzania wiedzą w organizacji. Prace Naukowe/Uniwersytet Ekonomiczny w Katowicach (2014)
4. Durst, S., Zieba, M.: Mapping knowledge risks: towards a better understanding of knowledge management. Knowl. Manag. Res. Pract. **17**, 1–13 (2018)
5. Kuah, C.T., Wong, K.Y., Tiwari, M.K.: Knowledge sharing assessment: an ant colony system based data envelopment analysis approach. Expert Syst. Appl. **40**(8), 3137–3144 (2013)
6. Mercier-Laurent, E., Rousseaux, F., Haddad, R.: Preventing and facing new crisis and risks in complex environments. Int. J. Manag. Decis. Making **17**(2), 148–170 (2018)
7. Przysucha, Ł.: Content management systems based on GNU GPL license as a support of knowledge management in organizations and business. In: Mercier-Laurent, E., Boulanger, D. (eds.) AI4KM 2015. IAICT, vol. 497, pp. 51–65. Springer, Cham (2016). https://doi.org/10.1007/978-3-319-55970-4_4
8. Pondel, M., Korczak, J.: Collective clustering of marketing data-recommendation system upsaily. In: 2018 Federated Conference on Computer Science and Information Systems (FedCSIS), pp. 801–810. IEEE (2018)
9. Przysucha, Ł.: Knowledge management in corporations–synergy between people and technology. Barriers and benefits of implementation. In: International Co-located Conferences (2017)
10. Owoc, M., Hołowińska, K.: Differentiation of supporting methods of business informatics teaching offered by selected educational portals. Informatyka Ekonomiczna **48**(2), 54–66 (2018). Wydawnictwo Uniwersytetu Ekonomicznego we Wrocławiu
11. Gołuchowski, J.: Inteligentne systemy diagnoz ekonomicznych. Prace Naukowe/Akademia Ekonomiczna w Katowicach (1997)
12. Owoc, M.L.: Wartościowanie wiedzy w inteligentnych systemach wspomagających zarządzanie. Prace Naukowe Akademii Ekonomicznej we Wrocławiu. Seria: Monografie i Opracowania 100 (1047) (2004)
13. Hernes, M.: Using cognitive agents for unstructured knowledge management in a business organization's integrated information system. In: Nguyen, N.T., Trawiński, B., Fujita, H., Hong, T.-P. (eds.) ACIIDS 2016. LNCS (LNAI), vol. 9621, pp. 344–353. Springer, Heidelberg (2016). https://doi.org/10.1007/978-3-662-49381-6_33
14. Kayakutlu, G., Mercier-Laurent, E.: From knowledge worker to knowledge cultivator-effective dynamics. In: Federated Conference on Computer Science and Information Systems (FedCSIS), pp. 1149–1153 (2012)
15. Davenport, T.H.: Improving knowledge worker performance. In: Pantaleo, D., Pal, N. (eds.) From Strategy to Execution, pp. 215–235. Springer, Heidelberg (2008). https://doi.org/10.1007/978-3-540-71880-2_11
16. Weichbroth, P., Brodnicki, K.: The lemniscate knowledge flow model. In: Federated Conference on Computer Science and Information Systems (FedCSIS), pp. 1217–1220. IEEE (2017). http://doi.org/10.15439/2017F357
17. Pancholi, S., Yigitcanlar, T., Guaralda, M.: Public space design of knowledge and innovation spaces: learnings from Kelvin Grove Urban Village, Brisbane. J. Open Innov. Technol. Mark. Complex. **1**(1), 13 (2015)

18. Kuciapski, M.: A model of mobile technologies acceptance for knowledge transfer by employees. J. Knowl. Manag. **21**(5), 1053–1076 (2017)
19. Przysucha, L.: Information management in the smart city-electronic tools facilitating the management of the metropolitan area. In: 2019 IEEE 10th International Conference on Mechanical and Intelligent Manufacturing Technologies (ICMIMT), pp. 189–193. IEEE (2019)
20. Sanin, C., Szczerbicki, E.: Towards the construction of decisional DNA: a set of experience knowledge structure java class within an ontology system. Cybern. Syst. **38**(8), 859–878 (2007)
21. Czarnecki, A., Sitek, T.: Ontologies vs. rules—comparison of methods of knowledge representation based on the example of IT services management. In: Information Systems Architecture and Technology: Intelligent Information Systems, Knowledge Discovery, Big Data and High Performance Computing, pp. 99–109 (2013)
22. Jarzębowicz, A., Markiewicz, S.: Representing process characteristics to increase confidence in assurance case arguments. In: Zamojski, W., Mazurkiewicz, J., Sugier, J., Walkowiak, T., Kacprzyk, J. (eds.) DepCoS-RELCOMEX 2019. AISC, vol. 987, pp. 245–255. Springer, Cham (2020). https://doi.org/10.1007/978-3-030-19501-4_24
23. Hauke, K., Owoc, M.L., Pondel, M.: Drążenie danych w środowisku Oracle 9i. Prace Naukowe Akademii Ekonomicznej we Wrocławiu, (955 Nowoczesne technologie informacyjne w zarządzaniu), pp. 315–330 (2002)
24. Lee, M.R., Chen, T.T.: Revealing research themes and trends in knowledge management: from 1995 to 2010. Knowl.-Based Syst. **28**, 47–58 (2012)
25. Ouriques, R.A.B., Wnuk, K., Gorschek, T., Svensson, R.B.: Knowledge management strategies and processes in agile software development: a systematic literature review. Int. J. Softw. Eng. Knowl. Eng. **29**(03), 345–380 (2019)
26. Quintas, P., Lefrere, P., Jones, G.: Knowledge management: a strategic agenda. Long Range Plan. **30**(3), 385–391 (1997)
27. Bergeron, B.: Essentials of Knowledge Management, vol. 28. Wiley, Hoboken (2003)
28. Barbaroux, P., Attour, A., Schenk, E.: Knowledge Management and Innovation: Interaction, Collaboration, Openness. Wiley, Hoboken (2016)
29. Marcinkowski, B., Gawin, B.: Project management in international IT ventures – does the practice go hand in hand with theory? In: Wrycza, S. (ed.) SIGSAND/PLAIS 2016. LNBIP, vol. 264, pp. 144–152. Springer, Cham (2016). https://doi.org/10.1007/978-3-319-46642-2_10
30. Polanyi, M.: Personal Knowledge: Towards a Post-Critical Philosophy. University of Chicago Press, Chicago (1958)
31. Owoc, M., Weichbroth, P., Żuralski, K.: Towards better understanding of context-aware knowledge transformation. In: Computer Science and Information Systems (FedCSIS), pp. 1123–1126. IEEE (2017). https://doi.org/10.15439/2017F383
32. Leonard, D., Sensiper, S.: The role of tacit knowledge in group innovation. Calif. Manag. Rev. **40**(3), 112–132 (1998)
33. Kaplanski, P., Weichbroth, P.: Cognitum ontorion: knowledge representation and reasoning system. In: Pełech-Pilichowski, T., Mach-Król, M., Olszak, Celina M. (eds.) Advances in Business ICT: New Ideas from Ongoing Research. SCI, vol. 658, pp. 27–43. Springer, Cham (2017). https://doi.org/10.1007/978-3-319-47208-9_3
34. Kapłański, P., Seganti, A., Cieśliński, K., Chrabrowa, A., Ługowska, I.: Automated reasoning based user interface. Expert Syst. Appl. **71**, 125–137 (2017)
35. Olszak, C., Mach-Król, M.: A conceptual framework for assessing an organization's readiness to adopt big data. Sustainability **10**(10), 3734 (2018)
36. Dixon, N.M.: Common Knowledge: How Companies Thrive by Sharing What They Know. Harvard Business School Press, Boston (2000)

37. Markus, M.L., Majchrzak, A., Gasser, L.: A design theory for systems that support emergent knowledge processes. MIS Q. **26**, 179–212 (2002)
38. Markus, L.M.: Toward a theory of knowledge reuse: types of knowledge reuse situations and factors in reuse success. J. Manag. Inf. Syst. **18**(1), 57–93 (2001)
39. Petty, R., Guthrie, J.: Intellectual capital literature review: measurement, reporting and management. J. Intell. Capital **1**(2), 155–176 (2000)
40. Rozkwitalska, M.: Employee learning in intercultural interactions-grounded theory. In: 10th Annual Conference of the EuroMed Academy of Business (2017)
41. Leja, K., Karwowska, E.: Tworzenie sieci współpracy uczelni z otoczeniem przy wykorzystaniu zamówień przedkomercyjnych na przykładzie projektu e-Pionier. e-mentor, **2**(69), 4–13 (2017)
42. Paralič, J., Babič, F., Paralič, M.: Process-driven approaches to knowledge transformation. Acta Polytechnica Hungarica **10**(5), 125–143 (2013)
43. Marcinkowski, B., Gawin, B.: A study on the adaptive approach to technology-driven enhancement of multi-scenario business processes. Inf. Technol. People **32**(1), 118–146 (2019)
44. Barafort, B., Shrestha, A., Cortina, S., Renault, A.: A software artefact to support standard-based process assessment: evolution of the TIPA framework in a design science research project. Comput. Stan. Interfaces **60**, 37–47 (2018)
45. Jawadekar, W.: Knowledge Management: Text & Cases. Tata McGraw-Hill, New Delhi (2010)
46. Awad, E.M., Ghaziri, H.M.: Knowledge Management. Prentice-Hall, New Jersey (2004)
47. Gołuchowski, J.: Technologie informatyczne w zarządzaniu wiedzą w organizacji. Prace Naukowe. Akademia Ekonomiczna w Katowicach (2007)
48. Fazlagić, J., Sikorski, M., Sala, A.: Portale intranetowe. Zarządzanie wiedzą, kapitał intelektualny, korzyści dla pracowników i dla organizacji. Politechnika Gdańska, Wydział Zarządzania i Ekonomii (2014)
49. Sikorski, M., Ludwiszewski, B., Fazlagic, J., Sala, A.: The impact of intranet portals on knowledge management in contemporary organizations. Probl. Zarzadzania **13**(52), 101–112 (2015)
50. Olszak, C.M., Ziemba, E.: Business intelligence systems in the holistic infrastructure development supporting decision-making in organizations. Interdisc. J. Inf. Knowl. Manag. **1**, 47–59 (2006)
51. Matouk, K., Owoc, M.L.: A survey of data warehouse architectures—preliminary results. In: Computer Science and Information Systems (FedCSIS), pp. 1121–1126. IEEE (2012)
52. Olszak, C.M.: Toward better understanding and use of business intelligence in organizations. Inf. Syst. Manag. **33**(2), 105–123 (2016)
53. Kapłański, P.: Controlled English interface for knowledge bases. Stud. Informatica **32**(2A), 485–494 (2011)
54. Kapłański, P.: Ontology-aided software engineering. Ph.D. thesis. Gdańsk University of Technology (2012)
55. Wróblewska, A., Kapłański, P., Zarzycki, P., Ługowska, I.: Semantic rules representation in controlled natural language in FluentEditor. In: 2013 6th International Conference on Human System Interactions (HSI), pp. 90–96. IEEE (2013)
56. Sussman, S.W., Siegal, W.S.: Informational influence in organizations: an integrated approach to knowledge adoption. Inf. Syst. Res. **14**(1), 47–65 (2003)
57. Nonaka, I.: A dynamic theory of organizational knowledge creation. Organ. Sci. **5**(1), 14–37 (1994)
58. Paliszkiewicz, J.: Knowledge management: an integrative view and empirical examination. Cybern. Syst. **38**(8), 825–836 (2007)

59. Weichbroth, P., Owoc, M., Pleszkun, M.: Web user navigation patterns discovery from WWW server log files. In: 2012 Federated Conference on Computer Science and Information Systems (FedCSIS), pp. 1171–1176. IEEE (2012)

60. Aviad, A., Węcel, K.: Cyber treat intelligence modeling. In: Abramowicz, W., Corchuelo, R. (eds.) BIS 2019. LNBIP, vol. 353, pp. 361–370. Springer, Cham (2019). https://doi.org/10.1007/978-3-030-20485-3_28

61. Efthymiou, K., Sipsas, K., Mourtzis, D., Chryssolouris, G.: On knowledge reuse for manufacturing systems design and planning: a semantic technology approach. CIRP J. Manufact. Sci. Technol. 8, 1–11 (2015)

62. Qin, H.: Design knowledge capture and reuse in an integrated and collaborative working environment. Doctoral dissertation, University of Portsmouth (2016)

63. Owen, J., Burstein, F., Mitchell, S.: Knowledge reuse and transfer in a project management environment. J. Inf. Technol. Cases Appl. 6(4), 21–35 (2004)

64. Sanin, C., Szczerbicki, E.: Dissimilar sets of experience knowledge structure: a negotiation process for decisional DNA. Cybern. Syst. 38(5–6), 455–473 (2007)

65. Shafiq, S.I., Sanin, C., Szczerbicki, E., Toro, C.: Virtual engineering factory: creating experience base for industry 4.0. Cybern. Syst. 47(1–2), 32–47 (2016)

66. Waris, M.M., Sanin, C., Szczerbicki, E.: Toward smart innovation engineering: decisional DNA-based conceptual approach. Cybern. Syst. 47(1–2), 149–159 (2016)

67. Baxter, D., Gao, J., Rajkumar, R.: Design process knowledge reuse challenges and issues. Comput. Aided Des. Appl. 5(6), 942–952 (2008). https://doi.org/10.3722/cadaps.2008.942-952

68. Gawin, B., Marcinkowski, B.: IT solutions integration: technical and organizational challenges. In: International Conference on ICT Management for Global Competitiveness and Economic Growth in Emerging Economies, pp. 111–123. University of Wrocław (2018)

69. Kowal, J., Keplinger, A., Mäkiö, J.: Organizational citizenship behavior of IT professionals: lessons from Poland and Germany. Inf. Technol. Dev. 25(2), 227–249 (2019)

70. Teufel, B.: Data encapsulation. In: Teufel, B. (ed.) Organization of Programming Languages, pp. 109–135. Springer, Vienna (1991). https://doi.org/10.1007/978-3-7091-9186-6_6

71. Weichbroth, P.: Fluent Editor and Controlled Natural Language in Ontology Development (2019, in Print)

72. Beesley, L.G., Cooper, C.: Defining knowledge management (KM) activities: towards consensus. J. Knowl. Manag. 12(3), 48–62 (2008)

73. Brown, C.: Critique and complexity: presenting a more effective way to conceptualise the knowledge adoption process. London Rev. Educ. 11(1), 32–45 (2013)

74. Pelc, M.: Context-aware fuzzy control systems. Int. J. Softw. Eng. Knowl. Eng. 24(05), 825–856 (2014)

75. Owoc, M., Weichbroth, P.: Validation model for discovered web user navigation patterns. In: Mercier-Laurent, E., Boulanger, D. (eds.) AI4KM 2012. IAICT, vol. 422, pp. 38–52. Springer, Heidelberg (2014). https://doi.org/10.1007/978-3-642-54897-0_3

76. Anjum, N., Harding, J., Young, R., Case, K., Usman, Z., Changoora, T.: Verification of knowledge shared across design and manufacture using a foundation ontology. Int. J. Prod. Res. 51(22), 6534–6552 (2013)

77. Chen, Y.-J.: Ontology-based empirical knowledge verification for professional virtual community. Behav. Inf. Technol. 30(5), 555–586 (2011)

78. Korczak, J., Dudycz, H., Nita, B., Oleksyk, P.: Towards process-oriented ontology for financial analysis. In: 2017 Federated Conference on Computer Science and Information Systems (FedCSIS), pp. 981–987. IEEE (2017)

79. Durcikova, A., Gray, P.: How knowledge validation processes affect knowledge contribution. J. Manag. Inf. Syst. 25(4), 81–108 (2009)

80. Dudycz, H.: Mapa pojęć jako wizualna reprezentacja wiedzy ekonomicznej. Monografie i Opracowania Uniwersytetu Ekonomicznego we Wrocławiu, no. 229 (2013)
81. Nguyen, T.A., Perkins, W.A., Laffey, T.J., Pecora, D.: Knowledge-base verification. AI Mag. **8**(2), 69–75 (1987)
82. Klein, M.C., Fensel, D.: Ontology versioning on the semantic web. In: SWWS, pp. 75–91 (2001)
83. Ventrone, V.: Semantic heterogeneity as a result of domain evolution. ACM SIGMOD Rec. **20**(4), 16–20 (1991)
84. Mach, M.A., Owoc, M.L.: Knowledge granularity and representation of knowledge: towards knowledge grid. In: Shi, Z., Vadera, S., Aamodt, A., Leake, D. (eds.) IIP 2010. IAICT, vol. 340, pp. 251–258. Springer, Heidelberg (2010). https://doi.org/10.1007/978-3-642-16327-2_31
85. Jakubczyc, J.A., Owoc, M.L.: Contextual knowledge granularity. In: Proceedings of Informing Science & IT Education Conference (InSITE), pp. 259–268 (2011)
86. Redlarski, K.: Hard lessons learned: a model that facilitates the selection of methods of IT project management. In: Federated Conference on Computer Science and Information Systems (FedCSIS), pp. 979–983. IEEE (2018)
87. Berztiss, A.T.: Reverse engineering, reengineering, and concurrent engineering of software. Int. J. Softw. Eng. Knowl. Eng. **5**(02), 299–324 (1995)
88. Prackwieser, C., Buchmann, R., Grossmann, W., Karagiannis, D.: Overcoming heterogeneity in business process modeling with rule-based semantic mappings. Int. J. Softw. Eng. Knowl. Eng. **24**(08), 1131–1158 (2014)
89. Owoc, M., Hauke, K., Weichbroth, P.: Knowledge-grid modelling for academic purposes. In: Mercier-Laurent, E., Boulanger, D. (eds.) AI4KM 2015. IAICT, vol. 497, pp. 1–14. Springer, Cham (2016). https://doi.org/10.1007/978-3-319-55970-4_1
90. Fensel, D.: Ontologies: Dynamic Networks of Formally Represented Meaning. Vrije University, Amsterdam (2001)
91. Lemoisson, P., Cerri, S.: Interactive knowledge construction in the collaborative building of an encyclopedia. Appl. Artif. Intell. **19**(9–10), 933–966 (2005)
92. Klein, O., Tamásy, C.: The ambivalence of geographic origin effects: evidence from the globalizing pork industry. Zeitschrift für Wirtschaftsgeographie **60**(3), 134–148 (2016)
93. Kothari, C.R., Russomanno, D.J.: Enhancing OWL ontologies with relation semantics. Int. J. Softw. Eng. Knowl. Eng. **18**(03), 327–356 (2008)
94. Flahive, A., Taniar, D., Rahayu, W., Apduhan, B.O.: Ontology tailoring in the semantic grid. Comput. Stand. Interfaces **31**(5), 870–885 (2009)
95. Maree, M., Belkhatir, M.: Addressing semantic heterogeneity through multiple knowledge base assisted merging of domain-specific ontologies. Knowl.-Based Syst. **73**, 199–211 (2015)

Modeling the Craftsmen Know-How: A Case Study Using MASK Methodology

Imane El Amrani[1(✉)], Abdelmjid Saka[1(✉)], Nada Matta[2(✉)],
and Taoufik Ouazzani Chahdi[1(✉)]

[1] National School of Applied Sciences of Fez, Quartier Industriel Ain Chkef,
Fez, Morocco
{imane.elamrani2, abdelmjid.saka}@usmba.ac.ma,
t.ouazzani@ueuromed.org
[2] University of Technology of Troyes, 12 Rue Marie Curie,
10010 Troyes, France
nada.matta@utt.fr

Abstract. Moroccan handicraft is rich in its know-how and authenticity, but today the informal way of transmitting knowledge loses its effectiveness. The risk of losing this cultural heritage because of competition and globalization challenges is real and its preservation is more necessary than ever. For that purpose, this paper aims to set up a capitalization process using knowledge management methods that are the best suited to be applied to this specific field. Presented here is a methodological framework divided into four big stages that are explained through a case study within the Moroccan zellige handicraft. The approach calls for identifying the most critical and vulnerable know-how and its transcription through a modeling approach. The methods used come from the knowledge management and knowledge engineering domains. We have chosen the MASK method for knowledge modeling and a mix between the "Process" approach and the "Domain" approach for the criticality study. The result is first and foremost a critical knowledge map of the proposed craft; and secondly, a transcription of the knowledge in the form of knowledge models that will compose a business memory currently missing in the handicrafts field.

Keywords: Knowledge engineering · Knowledge modeling · MASK ·
Moroccan handicraft · Handicrafts · Capitalization

1 Introduction

The Moroccan handicraft constitutes a rich and diversified cultural heritage. An ancestral heritage transmitted from generation to generation and from father to son through observation, imitation and practice. This is a tacit knowledge, rooted in action and routines and therefore difficult to formalize and transmit. A master craftsman acquires expertise derived from years of practice and experience, but he is often unable to describe the scientific rules or the technical principles relating to what he knows. When this transmission, which is inherently informal, deteriorates and loses its effectiveness two critical risks present themselves: (i) the vulnerability of this sector in relation to a crucial competence, which becomes increasingly rare, and (ii) a cultural

E. Mercier-Laurent and D. Boulanger (Eds.): AI4KM 2017, IFIP AICT 571, pp. 66–83, 2019.
https://doi.org/10.1007/978-3-030-29904-0_6

heritage is lost and the trade disappears. Hence the need to preserve the know-how of craftsmen in order to ensure its transmission and subsequently its sustainability.

To address this need, our study has been carried out with the objective of developing an appropriate and systematic approach based on MASK Method [1] in order to preserve the experiential knowledge of handicraftsmen in the form of a craft book that will be considered as reference in term of preservation of the handicrafts. However, most of the methods from the field of Knowledge Management and Knowledge Engineering have been designed within the formal world of industries and organizations. They require a high level of professionalization on the part of the actors involved in the capitalization process. MASK was chosen as it perfectly matches our objective in developing a book of knowledge besides its flexibility and easier ownership and especially its generic character [2] allowing it to adapt to different fields. However, some of its principles do not fit the world of craft and handedness. The crafts industry is governed by the informal in the absence of documentation and a low level of education making it difficult for the artisans to benefit from a formal capitalization process. In the light of this problem, a case study has been carried out to highlight the problems encountered and study the solutions to put in place. The case study is within the Moroccan zellige handicraft. A kind of clay mosaic hand cut in different shapes and colors that are imbricated to give shape to geometric decorations that will serve to cover the walls and floors. This ornamental technique is typical of Maghreb architecture and requires a very skilled and experienced handicraftsmen.

The approach addressed in this paper can be mainly divided into four steps: Building the process model, Identifying the critical knowledge, Capturing knowledge and finally modeling the critical knowledge. Every step is explained through the case study using concrete examples. The first two steps of the process give rise to a critical knowledge map that we have constructed in a simple diagram in order to enrich the book of knowledge. The approach behind building this map, although it's process-based at the beginning, is largely inspired by the "Domain" approach proposed by JL Ermines whose work is more present in the literature and is not lacking in detail and clarity especially when it comes to knowledge criticality assessment and representation. After collecting knowledge through observation and interviewing techniques, comes the last stage of modeling. MASK has been used for this purpose and the difficulties encountered are found more within the interviewing process with the expert craftsmen and the models co-construction principle besides the cultural barriers and reluctance to share.

The organization of this paper is as follows. It starts by a brief description of the state of the art and the study context followed by the presentation of the proposed approach and then its application to the case study within the Moroccan zellige craft. Finally, results are discussed; strengths and weaknesses of the methods used are addressed to conclude the paper.

2 Current State of the Art

In a cultural heritage context, the creation of a semantic representation of information and knowledge can be achieved effectively through the use of special diagrams. The most common ones are Ontologies such us the use of the CIDOC CRM template to derive the Architecture Metadata Object Schema for the cataloguing of architectural heritage [3, 4] or the traditional Malaya Textile knowledge model [5] or the ontology-based model developed within the conservation of the 6th-century San Saba oratory in Rome [4]. Others are using OWL ontologies, as in the case of Indian classical dance for the developement of a repository to preserve this intangible heritage [6]. However, these approaches are too domain-specific, especially adapted to the field of architectural heritage conservation during investigation activities and are therefore conceived for the design of an information technology system which can manage the big amount of data and information or a knowledge-based system (KBS) to reproduce inference mechanisms and build intelligent systems to assist with problem solving. The application within the handicraft domain is still lacking. Manfredi Latilla et al. [7] state that only 5 per cent of the total contributions analyzed in their literature review are focused on research within arts and craft organizations, while the big amount of contributions are dealing with organizations and technological firms in particular. Our goal is to capture the knowledge of the handicraftsmen using a modeling approach to produce models that are easily appropriable and directly exploitable to form a book of knowledge of the craft field.

A particular study has drawn our attention because it has many similarities with our case study in the way that it tends to formalize the tacit knowledge and operational know-how of the master craftsmen of Calabria in Italy [8]; The methodology used for acquiring and formalizing this knowledge is the CommonKADS standard as the ultimate goal is to develop a searchable and questionable expert system which will represent the cognitive process of experts in that craft sector. However, this method is located in a symbolic level and therefore use an adapted programming language rather than the knowledge level to which we limit ourselves in this paper.

Giving all the reasons mentioned above, MASK methodology [9] appeared to be the best suited to our case and this because of tree main reasons: (1) The knowledge representation format is based on a graphic modeling instead of a programming language, which makes it easy to build and read; (2) It makes it possible to constitute a business memory (book of knowledge) directly exploitable; (3) The interfering with the knowledge (the knowledge level) rather than the system (the symbolic level).

MASK method (Method for Analyzing and Structuring Knowledge), which used to be called MKSM (Method for Knowledge System Management, was invented at the CEA by the mathematician Jean-Louis Ermine [10]. It was used at the beginning to capitalize the knowledge of researchers approaching retirement in three particular areas: the nuclear tests, the fast neutrons and the laser enrichment of uranium [10]. It has been then extended to different sectors such as the textile industry and many other fields, namely the automotive industry such as the European giant Renault [11]. The goal of this method is to formalize knowledge from three perspectives that gave rise to six knowledge models [12]:

- A contextual point of view [12] giving rise to two models: the so-called "phenomenon models" where we seek to identify the phenomena underlying the knowledge and the "activity" model that is used to model the activities of the organization in which knowledge flows.
- A semantic point of view [12] giving rise to two other models: a so-called "task" (or "know-how") model which is a representation of the strategy or the expert reasoning used to solve a problem, and a "concept" model that represents the static aspect of knowledge.
- An evolutionary point of view [12] giving rise to the "historical" and "lineage" models which describe the evolution, first in its context, then in the sense (the lineages).

These models are developed during interviews with knowledge holders. They constitute a structured synthesis of knowledge on a given field called "Book of Knowledge" which is a kind of "business encyclopedia" [12]. It represents the final result of MASK methodology. The transition to a computer application (e.g. decision support system, database, etc.) is possible and immediate, using the models thus developed, which are considered to be sufficient and ready to use [12].

3 Study Context and Issue

In order to identify the specific issues related to this field, a case study was conducted within the Moroccan zellige craft that has led to identify the main characteristics describing the specificities of this field. The following points summarize the main characteristics of the Moroccan zellige craft:

- The nature of knowledge: an operational knowledge embedded in action, largely tacit and implicit and difficult to formalize.
- Informal learning: the transmission operates through observation and hands on experience; it's handed down from father to son and from master to novice
- Lack of documentation: an ancestral profession, which has been transmitted from generation to generation and from father to son in the family workshops secret without any formalization. Nevertheless, the work of the mathematician Jean Marc Castéra [13] or the architect Paccard [14] are discussing certain aspects of the Moroccan handicraft related to the design and the rules of geometric construction.
- Very poor level of education: most artisans didn't go to school and therefore do not have the necessary prerequisites to perform a formalization work.
- Difficulty in validating or co-constructing the models with the expert craftsmen: this is largely due to the lack of basic schooling; the majority of craftsmen have not attended school except of some privileged ones whom we have sometimes had the chance to meet.

4 Methodological Framework

The study context described above allowed us to build an appropriate approach to apprehend this case study that we describe in the diagram below (Fig. 1):

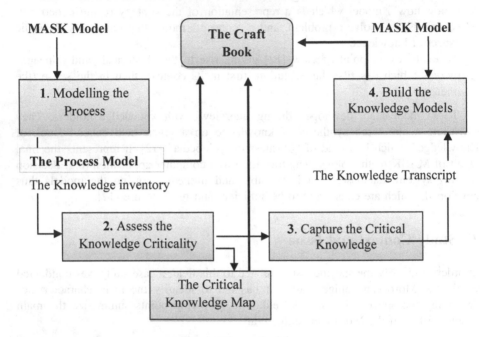

Fig. 1. The methodology.

In this section, the authors will describe the approach taken in this paper. Although it is at first glance obvious and generic in the description of its milestones, it has been the object of multiple revisions and corrections in order to adapt to the real context of the study. It is the result of a long observation in the field and several interviews conducted with stakeholders (artisans, regional delegation, trainers).

The first two stages of the process consist in the modeling of the processes followed by the evaluation of the knowledge criticality to produce two outputs: on the one hand a process model which will feed the craft book and on the other hand a critical knowledge map. The starting point of the methodology was initially the mapping of the critical knowledge in order to focus the capitalization effort on the most critical and vulnerable knowledge before moving on to the modeling process. However, the methods of knowledge mapping that we have studied in the literature, namely GAMETH Methodology [15] and M3C Methods [16] can't be systematically applied to our case study, an adaptation was necessary and led to a mix of the two approaches with a preliminary step of identifying knowledge from processes. This is why the authors have chosen as a starting point the modeling of the processes using MASK method which makes it possible to search the knowledge related to each activity and embedded in actions. This model has a double role; on the one hand it will be the first element, which will compose the trade book, and on the other hand, it makes it possible to identify the craft knowledge, which will be evaluated later to study their criticalities.

The M3C method is inspired from the work of the "Knowledge Management club" and is "Domains-oriented" approaches [16]. It calls for identifying knowledge areas based on the company's reference documents such as quality manuals and production documents, which are lacking in this field. The data harvesting technique for the criticality calculation is based on a structured interview with the expert who must assess the criticality level of the knowledge domains. But this very formal interview requires a high level of the interviewees' professionalization. On the other hand, the GAMETH method which is a process-driven and problem-driven approach [15] calls for identifying the essential processes and then the crucial activities in which critical knowledge is located. In the handicraft sector, tacitness is paramount in all of the process stages and a consensus is difficult to reach on identifying the most crucial production stages. Thus, the authors have selected from each of these two methods what best fit their case. From GAMETH, the process-based approach and from M3C the criticality calculation technique which will be explained in more detail in the case study. The authors have also proposed a knowledge map representation (inspired by Ishikawa in a process driven logic) (Fig. 7) and an interviewing process for the criticality assessment adapted to the artisans' profile (page 7).

Thus, after deciding what knowledge is most at risk, comes the stage of gathering this knowledge in order to formalize it through a modelling approach (step 3 and 4 of Fig. 1). The methods used for the knowledge elicitation are interviews and direct observation of the activity using video/audio recordings. The results of the interviews will be transcribed manually and then analyzed in relation to the different points of view defined by the MASK method (mentioned at the end of Sect. 2). This will make it possible to define the MASK models to be built, namely, the problem-solving model, the concept model, the historical model and the lineage models in addition to the process model already built in the first step.

5 Implementation of the Methodology Within the Moroccan Zellige Craft

The case study presented in this paper is within the Moroccan zellige craft. It is a type of handmade mosaic built from simple and basic materials (clay and enamels) using traditional tools that combined with the knobs and precision in the gesture give rise to multicolored geometric creations. The output is zellige panels that are placed on walls and floors and other various architectural elements in order to beautify them and give them more authenticity as shown in the following figure (Fig. 2). This craftsmanship can only be achieved through a long experience, practice and repeated observation of the master craftsman's gesture.

The approach presented above (Fig. 1) will thus be validated through this case study. The four steps will be covered one by one in the following with the aim of building a knowledge book for the preservation of this craft.

Fig. 2. An overview of the Moroccan zellige craft.

To conduct this field study, the authors have approached the Regional Delegation of Handicrafts in Fez city who recommended two master craftsmen recognized as experts in the field of zellige craft. It's about the expert craftsman "maâlem Benchekroun" and "maâlem Khalid Saib" who are also trainers at the handicraft training center in Fez. Their workshops were our target to closely observe the activity and to interview the artisans each in his specialty. Ten craftsmen with different levels of expertise were interviewed.

5.1 Step 1. Modeling the Process

The authors have chosen to represent the process model using the MASK method (Method of Analysis and Structuring Knowledge) which has been applied in a large number of domains [1] and [2]. This model as shown in Fig. 3, makes it possible to associate with each step of the process important elements for the accomplishment of the current activity such as the knowledge, the resources and the actors contributing to these activities. For this purpose, we have proceeded with interviews and videotaping, we have also resorted to some books such as "Arabesque" [13] and "*Le Maroc et l'artisanat traditionnel islamique dans l'architecture*" [14].

Fig. 3. An overview of the MASK process model

As it was said before, this process model has a double purpose, on the one hand it constitutes the first model that will compose our business memory which represents the ultimate goal of this work and on the other hand it will allow us to make an exhaustive inventory of the necessary knowledge to building the knowledge map (Fig. 4). The identification of the knowledge related to each activity of the process was the subject of a data gathering process based on interviews with the craftsmen. The main question that has been asked is the following: What do you think an artisan should know or be able to do, to accomplish this activity?. We have noticed over the interviews that asking a general question does not encourage the artisan to think and formulate his answer. It is preferable to go from general to specific and be more precise. We can say that we had have found the answer to our question in video recordings and direct observation rather than in the questioning exercise. The answer to our question was more about the tasks and the workflow process. Thus, for our case, the know-how related to the activity is assimilated to the tasks/sub-activities carried out.

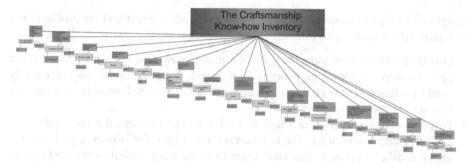

Fig. 4. The knowledge inventory extracted from the process model

5.2   Step 2. Assessing the Knowledge Criticality

The first step in assessing the knowledge criticality is the definition of the criticality grid. For this purpose, the authors used the generic evaluation grid called CKF (Critical Knowledge Factors) developed by the Knowledge Management Club [16]. Among the twenty criteria listed, the authors selected a dozen that fit perfectly into the context of the study. Topics covered included the rarity of knowledge holders and difficulties in acquiring and transmitting knowledge. The link with the strategy has also been considered in the criticality assessment. The following table (Table 1) presents the criteria we considered in this study.

After the definition of the criticality grid, comes the step for the criticality evaluation according to the criterion already defined. Ermine J-I. [17] has proposed a well-developed systematic approach for the criticality assessment study in which the levels of each criterion are carefully described and presented to the interviewee. Each assessment of criteria is based on a question. This systematic approach is certainly useful in facilitating the evaluation exercise. Nevertheless, it requires a high level of professionalization and abstraction on the part of the interviewees. For our case we

Table 1. The criticality grid.

Themes	Criteria
Rarity	1. Number and availability of holders 2. Confidentiality
Difficulty in acquiring knowledge	3. Difficulty in identifying sources 4. Knowledge taciteness 5. Availability of tangible sources of knowledge 6. Training time
Difficulty in using knowledge	7. Physical hardship 8. Level of expertise 9. Complexity 10. Difficulty in appropriation 11. Knowledge of history
Strategy	12. Adequacy with strategy

thought of a simplistic approach that best suits our study context and the profile of the evaluators (the artisans) as explained in the following steps.

1. Display the know-how using the craft jargon: the know-how elements defined in the previous step are copied on paper (post-it notes), using the vocabulary commonly used by artisans. These cards are presented to the master craftsman in an order that follows the process sequence.
2. Display only one criterion at a time and ask the expert to rank the knowledge in a criticality decreasing order: The criterion is chosen from the criticality grid, and the expert is asked to classify this knowledge from the most critical to the least critical according to this criterion. For example, for the criterion "Physical hardship", we asked the master craftsman to browse the notes and classify them from the hardest to the least hard by moving the cards on a column of four levels. Sometimes, the ranking is limited to just a few items, which means the criticality of the remaining know-how is negligible compared to those classified and could then be translated by a "0" rating.
3. Rate knowledge according to the ranking made by the expert: Each ranking level has a rating from 1 to 4, "4" for the most critical and "1" for the least critical as shown in Fig. 5. Thus the knowledge classified by the expert in the same Level will have the same notation and so on we will gather the results in a synthetic table.
4. Calculate the knowledge criticality: The criticality of each piece of knowledge is the weighted average of the criticality values for each criterion which is calculated by the following formula where "M" is the average of criticality values for each criterion [18].

$$M = \frac{\sum_i ki.Vcriterion}{\sum_i ki}$$

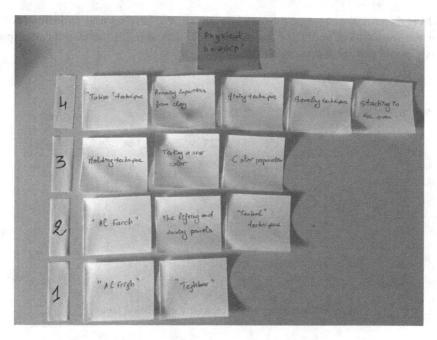

Fig. 5. An example of knowledge classification and ranking.

"Vcriterion" is the criticality value evaluated for each know-how and "ki" the weighting coefficient corresponding to criterion i whose value indicates the importance of the criterion as shown in Table 2.

Table 2. The criteria weighting coefficients value.

	Criteria	Weighting coefficient 'k'
C1	Number and availability of holders	2
C2	Confidentiality	1
C3	Difficulty in identifying sources	2
C4	Knowledge taciteness	2
C5	Availability of tangible sources of knowledge	2
C6	Training time	1
C7	Physical hardship	1
C8	Level of expertise	2
C9	Complexity	1
C10	Difficulty in appropriation	2
C11	Knowledge of history	1
C12	Adequacy with strategy	2

The following figure (Fig. 6) is an extract of the know-how criticality table calculation. On the lines we have the knowledge and on the columns the criticality criteria and M is the criticality average for each knowledge. We have set four criticality levels: 1 for the least critical and 4 for the most critical according to the classification previously performed by expert craftsman.

Criterion / Know-How	C1	C2	C3	C4	C5	C6	C7	C8	C9	C1	C1	C1	M
Testing a new color	(4)	4	(3)	(4)	3	2	4	4	3	4	4	4	**3.7**
Color preparation	4	4	3	4	3	3	4	4	3	3	2	2	**3.3**
'Takssir' Technique	1	0	0	4	1	4	4	4	4	0	2	4	**3.0**
The installation	1	3	0	4	4	3	4	4	3	0	1	1	**2.7**
The clay preparation	0	2	1	4	4	0	4	0	0	3	3	4	**2.7**
Stacking in the oven	1	1	1	4	3	4	4	2	2	1	1	1	**2.4**
'Tasstir' Technique	1	2	1	2	3	1	3	3	2	3	4	1	**2.3**

Number & Availability of holders — *Difficulty in identifying sources* — *Knowledge tacitness* — *Criticality average*

Fig. 6. An extract of the criticality calculation table.

The result of this first part of the study will be synthesized in the form of a critical knowledge map for which the authors have chosen a physical representation inspired from the Ishikawa diagram in a process-driven logic. Thereby the activities in the process model will constitute the map branches and the knowledge linked to each

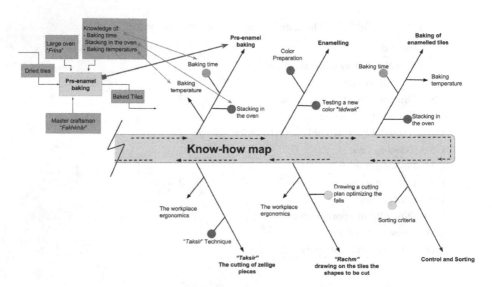

Fig. 7. An extract of the knowledge map (Color figure online)

activity will represent the sub-branches of the map as shown in the following diagram (Fig. 7).

In order to highlight the criticality level of the knowledge contained on the map, the authors chose three levels of criticality: a high level of criticality which includes 20% of the knowledge (red color), an average level that consists of 30% of knowledge (yellow color) and a low criticality level represented by 50% of the least critical knowledge (green color) (Fig. 7).

5.3 Step 3. Capturing the Critical Knowledge

Before starting a knowledge elicitation process with expert craftsmen, a preliminary analysis of the criticality table is required (Fig. 6). This analysis will make it possible to decide what knowledge can be transcribed in the form of a model. Thus, by crossing on each line the criticality value and on the column the nature of the criterion, it is possible to decide what action to put in place for a knowledge management plan including the knowledge modeling action. For instance, a knowledge which needs to be transcribed as a knowledge model will have a higher criticality according to criteria such as "Number and availability of holders", "Knowledge taciteness" or "Availability of tangible sources of knowledge". We have put some links on the process model to highlight the most critical elements in order to point to the knowledge models we need to build as shown in Fig. 8.

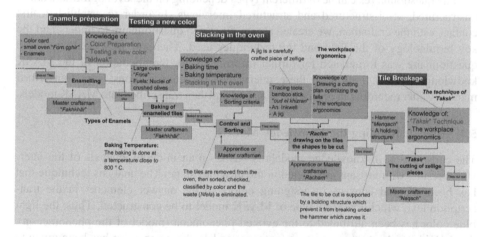

Fig. 8. The critical knowledge highlighted in the process model

Eliciting Knowledge from Experts

Many methods have been proposed through several researches addressing the issue of the knowledge acquisition/elicitation techniques. The first research and publications on the knowledge elicitation techniques appeared between 1985 and 2000 in scientific journals of knowledge engineering for the design and development of expert systems [19]. It was not until the 2000s (2000–2011) that a second wave of publications appeared and addressed the subject from a rather managerial point of view in scientific journals such as (Interdisciplinary Journal of Information, Knowledge & Management, Journal of Management Studies, Knowledge and Process Management, Human Resource Management, Journal of Knowledge Management,) [19]. It is therefore from the 2000s that researchers in the field of knowledge engineering were more interested in knowledge acquisition techniques not only for the development of intelligent systems but also for the knowledge management practices [19]. According to these works [19], the knowledge elicitation process can be divided into several levels according to the degree of knowledge formalization produced. A first level or a primary level includes methods such as: interviewing, observation method, storytelling, round table, brainstorming, role-playing, etc. The secondary level consists of methods that can only be applied after primary methods [19], such as repertory grids, rating, visual concept mapping and card sorting (visual concept mapping and card sorting), Etc.

In the handicraft field, the knowledge is largely operational and the work is totally manual with no formalization. The learning is done through practice and the transfer is completely oral. Thus, an upstream work of research on the field (Process, concepts, artefacts, processes, etc.) is necessary. For this purpose, the authors used books, documentaries and other data provided by the Ministry of handicrafts (studies, reports, surveys). After that, the authors have resorted to prolonged observations of the activity without addressing any questions to the artisans or interrupting him. Subsequently, interviews will be conducted to ask precise and focused questions based on the elements of the observation. This elicitation process is summarized in the Fig. 9.

The questionnaires can be of different types depending on the level of formalization: unstructured, semi-structured and structured interviews. In order to establish a first contact with the craftsman, we created a non-structured questionnaire to understand the key terminology of the field and the techniques used. Then, an additional structured questionnaire was formulated for further information for the elicitation of the MASK knowledge models. Following these interviews, the conversations were transcribed manually after recording in order to be analyzed and then transcribed into MASK models.

5.4   Step 4: Building the Knowledge Models

The construction of knowledge models is based on an in-depth analysis of the interviews results with artisans conducted in the previous stage. The analysis technique that has been adopted consists in assigning colors to the answer elements in the transcription text, which refer to a type of MASK model to be constructed. Thus, the light blue color has been attributed to the evoked phenomena (model of the phenomenon), the dark blue color to the processes (process model), the green color has been given to tasks and problem-solving operations (task model/problem solving) and finally the yellow for the concepts.

Among the models mentioned within the text of the interview transcript shown in the Fig. 10 below, three are presented in this paper, these are:

- The phenomenon model (Fig. 11) for the zellige tile "Breakage phenomenon",
- The Task/Problem solving model (Fig. 12) for the enameled tiles "Stacking in the oven",
- The Process model (Fig. 13) to define "The purification process" of the clay.

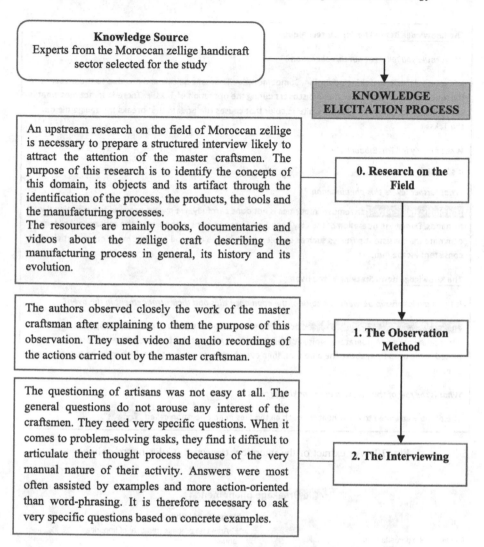

Fig. 9. The knowledge elicitation process

The Knowledge Item : The Takssir technique

What could you tell us about this operation?

It is a very delicate and tiring operation. Sometimes the tile breaks quickly and it is due to the presence of the wire in the cooked tiles that one discovers during the operation of Takssir. There is sometimes what is called Biboucha, generally appears white in color that causes the nouara that breaks the zellige tile during the Takssir.

What exactly is " The Biboucha"?

It's like limestone

What further favors this phenomenon ?

The purification process to remove impurities is not done carefully; we always proceed in a traditional way by hands. During the operation of the clay kneading, Legs and arms in the water, the artisan "ajjān" tries to eliminate the consistent particles such as pebbles, small pieces of wood etc., but many other particles less consistent escape him.

The Knowledge item. Stacking in the oven

Is there a relationship between the color of the enamelled tiles and their arrangement in the oven?

Their arrangement in the oven is staged according to the color so that each enamel is subjected to the appropriate baking temperature, white at the bottom and green at the top. The white tiles are always placed in the oven first, above the blue tiles, then even higher, the green tiles which must be less exposed to heat.

What is the role of this stacking in the baking process?

The tiles are arranged to allow heat to reach all the tiles in an operation called "Tedwar".

Fig. 10. An extract of the interview transcript (Color figure online)

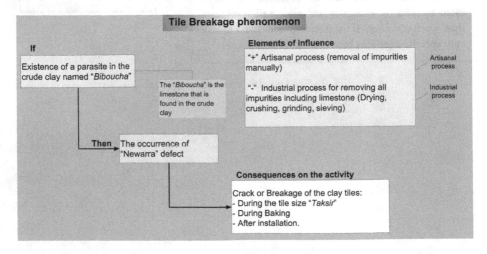

Fig. 11. The "Phenomenon Model" describing the tile breakage phenomenon.

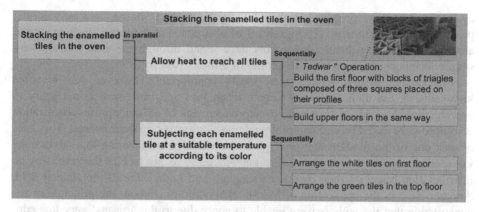

Fig. 12. The "Task/Problem solving" model for the "Stacking in the oven."

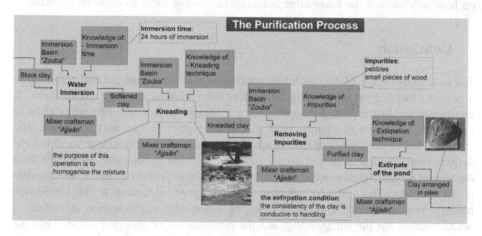

Fig. 13. The Process model for "The Purification Process".

6   Results and Discussion

The preservation of the Moroccan craftsmanship related knowledge is one of the strategic axis for the Moroccan handicraft preservation program. The study we have conducted in this paper constitutes a first step of this vision. The craft constraints make it difficult to systematically apply the methods that exist in the literature. These are often derived from the industrial world, which is completely different from the world of crafts. However, the application of MASK method has enriched this study and the results are promising. The first phase of the critical knowledge mapping revealed the very tacit aspect of knowledge and the inability of artisans to talk about what they know. Instead, they will talk about what they i.e. their operational knowledge, and this is how the authors agreed that knowledge will be assimilated to the activities and tasks of the process. This was the first proposal of the authors. The criticality evaluation that the master craftsman has to perform craftsmen has also been an issue. The criticality evaluation technique proposed in the M3C method [18] is based on a very formal process, which requires a very high level of abstraction and professionalism. In the absence of this prerequisite, the authors have tested through the case study a very simple technique that adapts to the profile of artisans (see page 7).

Finally, the MASK models were easily appropriate. However, having some knowledge of the trade (technical jargon, techniques and processes) is necessary to apprehend such a project in order to overcome the lack of artisan's professionalization who need to be asked precise and profound questions to stir up their interest. This goes against one of the fundamental principles of knowledge engineering that advises the knowledge engineer to come with zero knowledge so as not to bias the results by an interpretation based on their own understanding and knowledge of the studied field. Another issue in the application of MASK methodology is about the principle of co-construction that the authors were unable to apply due to the artisans' very low education level. Thus, this project has raised many challenges and needs a real reflection on how to interview the knowledge holders and involve them more in this process.

7 Conclusion

The case study on the Moroccan zellige profession that we carried out and presented in this paper has led up to building an approach for cultural heritage preservation. It constitutes a coherent basis for apprehending a similar project. The one we propose in this article is subject to improvement. It can be further refined and improved. The difficulty lies in the knowledge harvesting technique and the knowledge models validation. The experts interviewed do not meet the required prerequisites to benefit from the formal capitalization process and the co-construction process of the MASK models is not possible. This must be reflected and redesigned according to the knowledge holders' profile. Critical know-how requiring knowledge capitalization constitutes a priority action for the safeguarding and the perpetuation of this profession. Thus we have opted for the knowledge modeling using the MASK methodology in order to build an Electronic Book of Knowledge that will constitute a business memory currently missing.

References

1. Ermine, J.L.: Capitaliser et partager les connaissances avec la méthode MASK. Hermès, Paris (2001)
2. Matta, N., Ermine, J.L., Aubertin, G., Trivin, J.Y.: Knowledge Capitalization with a Knowledge Engineering Approach: The Mask Method. In: Management, Knowledge, Memories, Organizational (eds.) Dieng-Kuntz R, Matta N, pp. 17–28. Springer, Boston (2002). https://doi.org/10.1007/978-1-4615-0947-9_2
3. Agathos, M., Kapidakis, S.: A meta - model agreement for architectural heritage. In: Garoufallou, E., Greenberg, J. (eds.) Metadata and Semantics Research, pp. 384–395. Springer, Cham (2013). https://doi.org/10.1007/978-3-319-03437-9_37

4. Acierno, M., Cursi, S., Simeone, D., Fiorani, D.: Architectural heritage knowledge modelling: an ontology-based framework for conservation process. J. Cult. Heritage **24**, 124–133 (2017)
5. Nasir, S.A.M., Noor, N.L.M., Razali, S.: The traditional malay textile (TMT) knowledge model: transformation towards automated mapping. World Acad. Sci. Eng. Technol. **4**, 716–721 (2010)
6. Mallik, A., Chaudhury, S., Ghosh, H.: Nrityakosha: Preserving the intangible heritage of Indian classical dance. J. Comput. Cult. Heritage (JOCCH) **4**(3), 11 (2011)
7. Manfredi Latilla, V., Frattini, F., Messeni Petruzzelli, A., Berner, M.: Knowledge management, knowledge transfer and organizational performance in the arts and crafts industry: a literature review. J. Knowl. Manag. **22**(6), 1310–1331 (2018)
8. Guarasci, R., Cosentino, A., Cardillo, E., Folino, A., Taverniti, M.: Gestion et formalisation de la connaissance tacite des maîtres-artisans de la Calabre (Doctoral dissertation, Università della Calabria-Laboratorio di Docuemtazione) (2008)
9. Matta, N., Ermine, J.L., Aubertin, G., Trivin, J.Y.: How to capitalize knowledge with the MASK method. In : IJCAI 2001 Workshop on Knowledge Management and Organizational Memories, vol. 6, August 2001
10. Prax, J.Y.: Le manuel du Knowledge Management: une approche de 2e génération. Dunod, Paris (2003)
11. Castillo, O., Matta, N., Ermine, J.L.: De l'appropriation des connaissances vers l'acquisition des compétences. In: 2ème colloque C2EI: Modélisation et pilotage des systèmes de Connaissances et de Compétences dans les Entreprises Industrielles, pp. 1–8, December 2004
12. Aries, S., Le Blanc, B., Ermine, J.L.: MASK: une méthode d'ingénierie des connaissances pour l'analyse et la structuration des connaissances (2008)
13. Castera, J.M., Peuriot, F.: Arabesques: art décoratif au Maroc. Art, Création et Réalisation, ACR (1996)
14. Paccard, A.: Le Maroc et l'artisanat traditionnel islamique dans l'architecture. Atelier 74 (1983)
15. Grundstein, M., Rosenthal-Sabroux, C.: Une aide à la décision pour le repérage des connaissances potentiellement cruciales dans un projet de conception: application du cadre directeur GAMETH®. Gestion dynamique des connaissances industrielles, pp. 81–106 (2004)
16. Tounkara, T., Ermine, J.L.: Méthodes de Cartographie pour l'alignement stratégique de la gestion des connaissances (2008)
17. Ermine, J.L.: Valoriser les connaissances les connaissances critiques d une entreprise (2004)
18. Ermine, J.L., Boughzala, I., Tounkara, T.: Critical knowledge map as a decision tool for knowledge transfer actions. Electron. J. Knowl. Manag. **4**(2), 129–140 (2006)
19. Gavrilova, T., Andreeva, T.: Knowledge elicitation techniques in a knowledge management context. J. Knowl. Manag. **16**(4), 523–537 (2012)

Knowledge Extracting from Eco-Design Activity

Nada Matta[✉], Tatiana Reyes, and Florian Bratec

ICD, University of Technologie of Troyes, Troyes, France
{nada.matta,tatiana.reyes,florian.bratec}@utt.fr

Abstract. The integration of eco-design in industries is becoming more and more considered as a necessary condition of Sustainable development. It should be noted that the consideration of environmental issues in design can modify the objectives, outputs, resources, processes and performance indicators of a company. Eco-design goals (using of renewable materials, recycling, reducing energy, etc.) coupled with economic and social objectives (implication of stakeholders, sharing knowledge, considering culture aspect, etc.) are more or less considered in proactive or prescriptive way. These approaches lead to develop innovative solutions (circular economy, hybrid energy production, etc.). Even some rules are identified for sustainability but the application of these rules still no common in industries. Each industry try to understand these rules and apply some of them. The relationships between technical, economical and organizational aspects still undetermined. In this paper, extracting knowledge from the applications of sustainability rules in industries is presented as a way to share eco-design indicators. This first studies will help to define concept models of eco-design which help to extract indicators from documents and guide designers to consider environment criteria an evaluate their design.

Keywords: Design projects · Traceability · Classifications

1 Introduction

The integration of eco-design in industries is becoming more and more considered as a necessary condition of Sustainable development. It should be noted that the consideration of environmental issues in design can modify the objectives, outputs, resources, processes and performance indicators of a company. Eco-design goals (using of renewable materials, recycling, reducing energy, etc.) coupled with economic and social objectives (implication of stakeholders, sharing knowledge, considering culture aspect, etc.) are more or less considered in proactive or prescriptive way. These approaches lead to develop innovative solutions (circular economy, hybrid energy production, etc.). We can note that eco-design joins the environmental innovation logic [5, 17] allowing to reduce material and energy impact.

The integration of environmental issues in design was clearly identified by Victor Papanek in his book 'Design for the Real World: Human Ecology and Social Change' [19]. The 70's is a period characterized by a growing interest in environmental studies to support innovative design: Coca-Cola was the first company to realize a multi-

Published by Springer Nature Switzerland AG 2019
E. Mercier-Laurent and D. Boulanger (Eds.): AI4KM 2017, IFIP AICT 571, pp. 84–98, 2019.
https://doi.org/10.1007/978-3-030-29904-0_7

criteria study to assess the environmental impacts related to the production and the end-of-life of their product [8]. The method is based on the whole life-cycle of the product: from the raw materials extraction to the end-of-life treatment of the product, considering as well the steps of supplying, production, distribution, use and maintenance [10]. This methodology is now part of the ISO14000 environmental management standard since 2006.

Even some rules are identified for sustainability but the application of these rules still no common in industries. Each industry try to understand these rules and apply some of them in companies. The relationships between technical, economical and organizational aspects still undetermined. In this paper, extracting knowledge from the applications of sustainability rules in industries is presented as a way to share eco-design indicators. For this aim, several techniques are used: extracting criteria from documents, extracting decision making concepts from cooperative eco-design projects and identifying domain concepts from expertise. A draft of eco-design domain ontology is built from these studies.

2 Extracting Eco-Design Criteria from Documents

As first steps of this study, design indicators can be identified from analysing experience feedback. Therefore, expertise documents gathered in a young company, containing design data about materials and processes, are analysed. We show in this section how the features defining these materials and processes have been identified.

2.1 Expertise Documents

Altermaker is a young start-up specialized in software development to support design for sustainability. The company led analysis on industrial materials and processes used in mechanical engineering. The results are stocked as MsPowerpoint documents in which several elements are defined for each material or process: advantages, disadvantages, short description and specific comparisons. In these documents (Fig. 1), several features are interesting to consider and other ones need more analysis. Our study aims at analysing these documents in order to define the concepts that show the main features of given materials and processes.

2.2 Analysing Approach

Knowledge engineering techniques [21] are used to analyse Altermaker documents. In this type of approach, expertise documents can be analysed in order to identify the role that elements can play in problem solving related to a specific domain, what is called concepts. Several techniques can be used in documents analysis, we note especially TextMining [7] that is based on repetition of words and on relations between words. In this study, each slide presents a specific material or process. Therefore, using automatic TextMining tools cannot be interesting in our case: documents should be analysed manually.

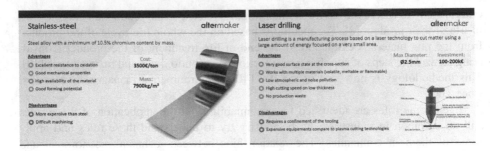

Fig. 1. Example of Altermaker documents (material card and process card)

In total, 80 slides are analysed for materials and 157 for processes. Processes documents are already classified on manufacturing, assembling and cutting. But there is no classification of materials slides. Analysing steps, the procedure can be summarised as:

1. Characteristics are identified from description, advantages and disadvantages (Fig. 2)
2. The number of occurrences of characteristics are counted
3. Results are then presented to two mechanical eco-design experts of Altermaker in order to eliminate noise, conflicts and to validate the relevance of each characteristic
4. Characteristic categories are detailed and split in sub-groups
5. Groups are then validated by the eco-design experts
6. Finally, analysing of omissions in order to possibly complete classifications (Fig. 3).

2.3 Characteristics Classifications

Repetition of characteristics is then used in order to classify them. On one hand, our classification aims at emphasizing the impact of process and materials on the environment and, on another hand, at helping designers to deal with process and materials in eco-design. For instance, the main process characteristics are identified as: cost, consummation, pollution, technicality, etc. (Fig. 4).

For materials, we identify: Resistance, compacity, disassembling, modification, etc. (Fig. 5). Then, for each process type (assembling, drilling, welding, …) values are associated to these classifications.

These identified characteristics and classifications allowed us to build a database of processes and materials with technical, organisational and economic data. These characteristics are then linked to environmental ones and ready to be implemented in the "ECODESIGN STUDIO"[1] software to support decision making of environmental experts.

Besides this analysis, some eco-design projects are analysed. These projects are realized by students in our university. The following section presents this analysis.

---

[1] http://www.altermaker.com/fr/.

Characteristics	Slides	Repetition	Pourcentag
Acceptance misalignment	373, 374	2	20%
Adjustment of pieces with fine contact	372	1	10%
Automatization	367	1	10%
need other process	370	1	10%
Rapidity	367, 370, 372, 374, 376	5	50%
Innovative concept	372	1	10%
Constraints of temperature (after assembly)	376	1	10%
temperature control	367	1	10%
Quality control	367	1	10%
Cost	376	1	10%
Unusally Distortion	376	1	10%
Disassembling	373, 374	2	20%

Fig. 2. Example of identified first 45 characteristics for Tube assembling.

Process Types	Nb slides	Nb characteristics					
		Step 1	Step 2	Step 3	Step 4	Step 5	Step 6
		Ident. characs	statisitics	Validation 1	Splitting	Validation 2	Missing
Manufacturing	68	113	113	28	33	32	25
Assembling Tubes	6	45	45	20	23	21	20
Assembling Tubes	47	115	115	52	55	51	39
Heatting	7	23	23	19	20	19	17
Micro-drilling	5	22	22	15	15	15	14
Micro-manufacturing	6	20	20	15	16	14	14
drilling	12	26	26	17	19	19	16
Contacted joins	6	22	22	18	18	18	17
	157						

Fig. 3. Results of process documents analysing.

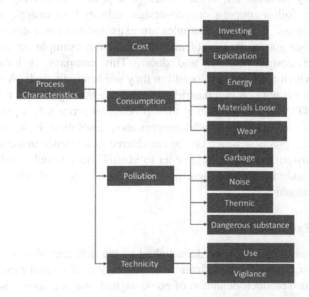

Fig. 4. Example of process characteristics

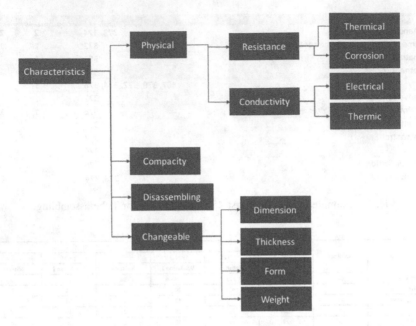

Fig. 5. Example of materials characteristics

3 Extracting Knowledge from Eco-Design Projects

In our university students are asked to design a product respecting environmental constraints. They follow course about eco-design and they have to apply studied theory in simulated projects. The given examples are extracted from real company (as wooden, forge, leather goods, etc.) problems. We study the example on wooden factory "SANTIN" that design windows and doors. This company is located in Aube department in which there are two forest but they use foreign woods. A river cross the department which is not rich in industries. Considering the big competition in this type of factory, SANTIN aim at innovating their production process by opening it to eco-design. Students are then invited to brainstorm about a solution. First, they are invited to look to existing products which can be considered as reference in their analysis. We study their brainstorming meetings in order to identify operational eco-design criteria. Our aim is to study how eco-design theory can be transformed with which type of criteria at operational level.

3.1 Project Execution

Eight brainstorming meetings are done linked to the different phases of the project: existing analysis, problems identification, Identification of related products, Identification of reference product, definition of eco-designed product, comparison of the two products. One additive meeting has been done in order to identify the organization of the project, its finality and a schedule. A report summarizing the project execution and the eco-designed product characteristics has been written. The teacher played the role of environmental expert who guides students to consider environment parameters. Students coming from mechanical design and building design play the role of eco-designers.

3.2 Project Analysis

Meetings are recorded using MMRecord tablet applications [16]. This application help to record discussions related to questions and participants (Fig. 6).

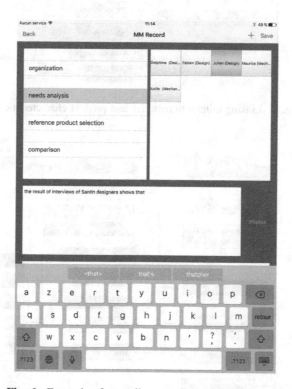

Fig. 6. Example of recording meetings with MMRecord

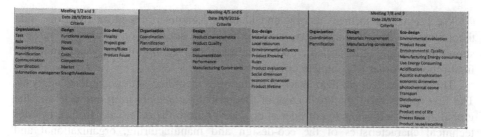

Fig. 7. Example of criteria identified from project meetings

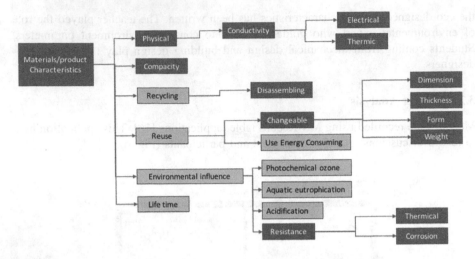

Fig. 8. Linking criteria to material and product characteristics

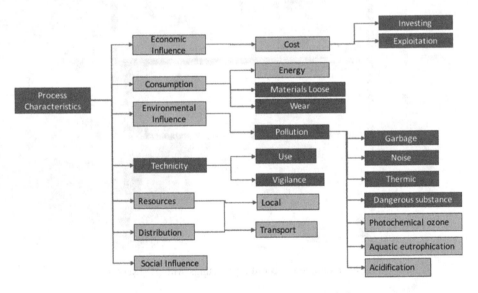

Fig. 9. Linking criteria to process characteristics

We listen then to these records and identify parameters based on from one side theoretical eco-designs parameters, design criteria and organisation indicators. Figure 7 shows an example of identified criteria from meetings. Adding of that, we examine the final report in order to complete our analysis.

These parameters are then attached to the ones identified with documents analysis. The first results show the application of theoretical parameters from one side and the global view of indicators to consider in eco-design from the other side. In fact, besides technical characteristics of the eco-design and manufacturing, organizational and economical ones must be considered (Figs. 8 and 9).

This first studies will help to define concept models of eco-design which help to extract indicators from documents using TextMining, when considering the model as lexicon, from one side and guide designers to consider environment criteria in eco-design projects by using then in evaluation. This work is first step toward a definition of an ontology in eco-design. The following sessions present the collection of concepts from domain experts and scientific papers for this aim.

4 Eco-Design Ontology

There are different works that define ontologies for eco-design. These ontologies are specific to some applications like biorafinery [13] or specific problems as linking raw materials to products [9], or LCA process [12, 14]. Other ones identify emphasize environment main concepts linked to eco-design [11]. In our study, generic ontology is used in order to gather the main concepts in theses ontologies and to identify a domain one as a guide for eco-designers. So, we proceed by an overall approach studying main works in this domain. To define this type of type of ontology, two approaches are used:

- top-down by interviewing experts and defining main concepts structuring the ontology
- bottom-up by extracting concepts from scientific papers, in the domain using Textming technique [2].

4.1 Experts Interviewing

Two eco-design experts have been interviewed. These experts help different industries in the last 3 years. They are also involved in sustainability research. We use Knowledge engineering techniques and we co-build with them the main structures of eco-design ontology. Related to Dolce generic ontology, we identify three types of concepts (Fig. 10):

- Endurant which describes substances, row materials and Energy
- Perdurant related to design activities (Fig. 10) as: raw materials, manufacturing, packaging, distribution, use and recycling.
- Abstract which help to defines influence and changing facts as: Depletion, Transformation, specialization, destroying and consequences (Fig. 10).

The main eco-design activity is to identify how Perdurant (design activity) disturbs Endurant (environment) based on the Abstract influence relations. So, a graph is defined in order to emphasize these influences (Fig. 11). This type of influences is also noted by Ostad [14] when analysing the relation of LCA with the environment.

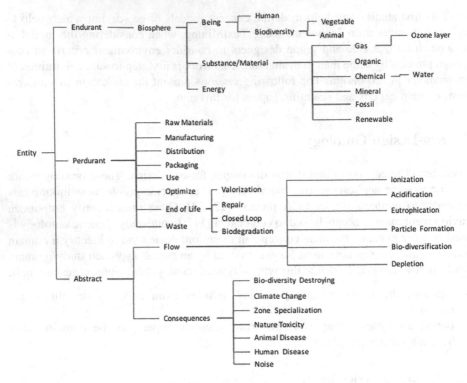

Fig. 10. Eco-design ontology

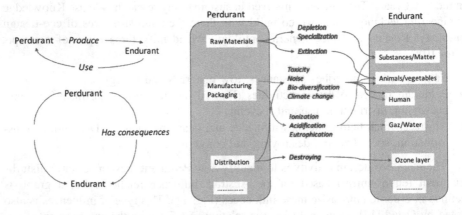

Fig. 11. When Perdurant disturbs Endurant

5   Extracting Concepts from Scientific Papers

38 Eco-design papers, published on ICED 2017, are analysed. The "Voyant Tool" Textmining [2] tool[2]; has been applied on papers related to each topic and a list of terms has been identified.

5.1   Terms Analysis

Firstly, a selection of papers has been done using the term "ecodesign" from ICED2019 proceedings. 38 papers were found. Then the TextMining Tool "Voyant tool" (See footnote 2) has been applied on one time on these documents without any categorization or indication of preferred words 191 occurrences of terms has been identified. After cleaning of usual terms: 69 words are identified related to eco-design. Single and plural terms are then gathered and we obtain 47 terms. Figure 12 shows the number of occurrence of these terms in analysed papers.

Voyant tool shows also relationships between terms in the text based on the existence of terms in the same sentence or paragraph. So, we apply this tool on each paper and we gather links between terms in one graph (Fig. 13).

5.2   Concepts Identification

Concepts are then defined from terms based on the structure if the ontology built with the expert. That help to confirm some concepts and to add other ones. Figures 14 and 15 illustrate this augmented ontology.

These results show that currently several works study process and technologies to enhance eco-design life cycle. Some papers deal with management, economy and social aspects. Behaviour and learning dimensions are also mentioned. The number of these keywords on ICED 2017 proceedings show that the sensibility of research on human, social and economic subjects is not largely developed. The model proposed by Ceschin et al. 2016 shows that the Design For Sustainability (DFS) approaches have progressively extended from technological aspects to human and from unique products to complex systems in a systemic vision [3]. This means that the skills and role of eco-designers have evolved. The work of Millet et al. shows that the eco-designer must have scientific (design, environmental, sustainability and value chain), legal and DFS tools skills [18]. The ontology Fig. 14 shows us that eco-designer nowadays must also have inventive, visionary and troubleshooting capabilities to address sociotechnical issues. The ecodesign must play the role of «cultural intermediary» (in the sense of [20] of the dissemination of DFS knowledge and creator of a stakeholders' network throughout the value chain of a system over one or more life cycles.

We will continue our exploration and study journals papers in sustainability and eco-design in order to enrich this type of ontology and emphasize dimension to consider in DFS.

---

[2] https://voyant-tools.org/.

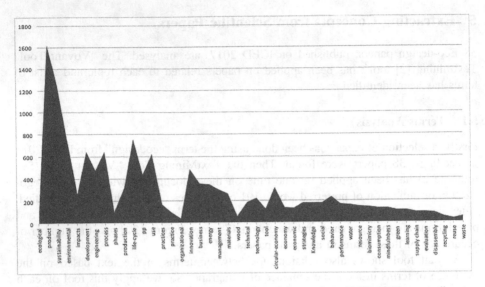

Fig. 12. Occurrence of eco-design terms in selected papers from ICED 2017 proceedings.

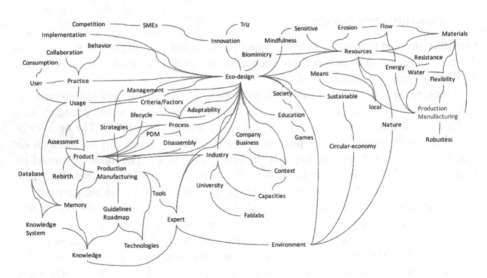

Fig. 13. Links between terms found in selected papers from ICED 2017 proceedings

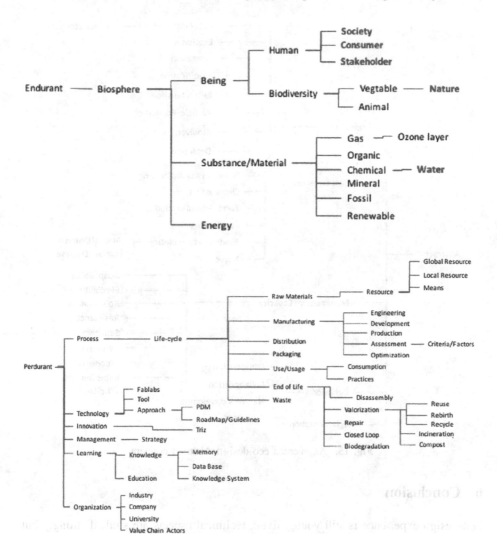

Fig. 14. Augmented eco-design Perdurant and Endurant concepts

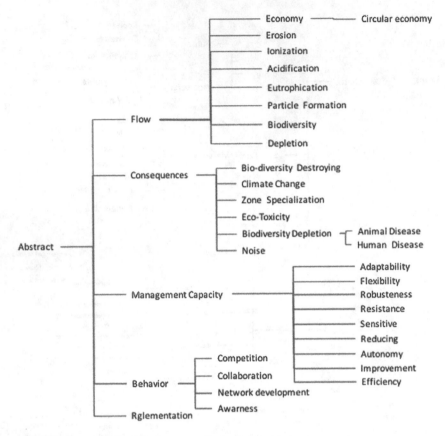

Fig. 15. Augmented eco-design Abstract concept

6 Conclusion

Eco-design experience is still young. Even, technical aspects are studied strongly but there is no consolidation of the relationships between technical and organizational and economical dimensions. We try in this paper to explore this relationships by extracting concepts from using two approaches: related to TextMining from documents and traceability of projects. We obtained criteria in different level of abstraction. As same as, we prove the feasibility of these techniques even there is no big documentation in eco-design (mainly from scientific research) and projects still very innovative. First concepts defined can help us as a lexicon to use TextMining in automatic way and as guides to help in eco-design projects. This work is a first step towards definition of a knowledge Base for eco-design. That can help designers to mainly integrate a green approach in their activity. The eco-design ontology can be considered as a guide in order to define models for specific activities. Main concepts shown in this ontology put on the influence type of production activity on the environment. This work is not exhaustive and eco-design ontology can be completed either from ongoing studies or real applications and studying other scientific papers. We aim at continuing our analysis of eco-design projects using DYPKM [1, 15] traceability approach and KDR [4] classification technique in order to identify more criteria at operational level. Students continue to use MMProject application and keep track of their project execution.

Otherwise, we explore territory literature and design organizational supply chain in order to open eco-design studies to organizational and social dimensions. We hope at the end of this studies to define an ontology of main indicators to help eco-design evaluation process and products. First has been so defined emphasizing from one side materials and natural flows and social and informational organization from another side.

First results will be integrated in eco-design tool the "ECODESIGN STUDIO"[3] that allow to validate our hypothesis in real projects.

References

1. Bekhti, S., Matta, N.: A formal approach to model and reuse the project memory. J. Univ. Comput. Sci. (JUCS) **6** (2003)
2. Berry, M.W., Castellanos, M.: Survey of Text Mining II, vol. 6. Springer, New York (2018). https://doi.org/10.1007/978-1-84800-046-9
3. Ceschin, F., Gaziulusoy, I.: Evolution of design for sustainability: from produt design to design for system innovations ad transitions. Des. Stud. **2016**(47), 118–163 (2016)
4. Dai, X., Matta, N., Ducellier, G.: Cooperative knowledge discovery in design projects. In: IC3 K, Knowledge Management and Information System Conferences, Rome, October 2014
5. Depret, M.H., Hamdouch, A.: Quelles politiques de l'innovation et de l'environnement pour quelle dynamique d'innovation environnementale? Innovations **1**, 127–147 (2009)
6. Dewulf, W.: Design for sustainability-anticipating the challenge. In: DS 31: Proceedings of ICED 2003, the 14th International Conference on Engineering Design, Stockholm (2003)
7. Feldman, R., Sanger, J.: The Text Mining Handbook: Advanced Approaches in Analyzing Unstructured Data. Cambridge University Press, Cambridge (2007)
8. LCA—How it came about. Int. J. Life Cycle Assess. **1**(1), 4 (1996)
9. Houe, R., Grabot, B.: Knowledge modeling for eco-design. Concur. Eng. **15**(1), 7–20 (2007)
10. Knight, P., Jenkins, J.O.: Adopting and applying eco-design techniques: a practitioner's perspective. J. Clean. Prod. **17**(5), 549–558 (2009)
11. Kumazawa, T., et al.: Knowledge structuring process of sustainability science based on ontology engineering. In: Proceedings of the 8th International Conference on Eco Balance, Tokyo, Japan, pp. 409–412 (2008)
12. Lim, S.R., Park, J.M.: Environmental indicators for communication of life cycle impact assessment results and their applications. J. Environ. Manag. **90**(11), 3305–3312 (2009)
13. Lousteau-Cazalet, C., et al.: A decision support system for eco-efficient biorefinery process comparison using a semantic approach. Comput. Electron. Agric. **127**, 351–367 (2016)
14. Ostad-Ahmad-Ghorabi, H., Bey, N., Wimmer, W.: Parametric ecodesign–an integrative approach for implementing ecodesign into decisive early design stages. In: DS 48: Proceedings DESIGN 2008, the 10th International Design Conference, Dubrovnik, Croatia (2008)
15. Matta N, Atifi H, Ducellier G: Daily Knowledge Valuation in Organizations. Willey (2016)

---

[3] http://www.altermaker.com/fr/.

16. Matta, N., Ducellier, G.: How to learn from design project knowledge. Int. J. Knowl. Learn. **9**(1–2), 164–177 (2014)
17. Michelin, F., Vallet, F., Reyes, T., Eynard, B., Duong, V.L.: Integration of environmental criteria in the co-design process: case study of the client/supplier relationship in the French mechanical industry. In: Proceedings of the DESIGN 2014 13th International Design Conference, Dubrovnik, pp. 1591–1600 (2014)
18. Millet, D., Coopens, C., Jaqueson, L., Le Borgne, R., Tonnelier, P.:   Intégration de l'environnement en conception. Hermes, Paris (2003)
19. Papanek, V.: Design for the real world: human ecology and social change (1971)
20. Santamaria, L., Escobar-Tello, C., Ross, T.: Switch the channel: using cultural codes for designing and positioning sustainable products and services for mainstream audiences. J. Cleaner Prod. **123**, 16–27 (2016)
21. Studer, R., Benjamins, V.R., Fensel, D.: Knowledge engineering: principles and methods. Data Knowl. Eng. **25**(1), 161–197 (1998)

Representing Stress Impact in Crisis Management

Sammy Teffali[✉], Nada Matta[✉], and Eric Chatelet[✉]

Université de Technologie de Troyes, 12 rue Marie Curie, BP. 2060,
10010 Troyes, Cedex, France
{sammy.teffali,nada.matta,eric.chatelet}@utt.fr

Abstract. The crisis management is a special type of collaborative approach in which the actors are subject to an uninterrupted stress. It is quite a significant issue because the consequences of crises can bring huge damages (human and economic losses). Even actors follow training in order to face stress situations but the human condition (familial and life) and the disparity of situations in which the consequences (different types of victims (children, the elderly, etc.) push actors to lose control of situations. The question to answer is can we predict the consequence of a default to this type of situation? Our study try to answer these questions by showing how to represent prediction of the consequences of a stress on crisis management. Firstly, we define a model that represents the impact of one actor to the situation considering the collaborative aspect of crisis and then we study stress consequences measurement. First results of these studies are presented in this paper.

Keywords: Crisis management · Stress · Prediction

1 Introduction

Crisis management is a special type of collaborative approach in which the actors are subject to an uninterrupted stress. It requires succeeding because the consequences are important (human and economic losses). We study the management of crises in the case of disasters, heavy accidents or sanitary alerts (poor meteorological conditions, terrorism, etc.). The multiplicity of actors, the importance of the consequences (deaths, serious injuries), the complexity and the disparity of situations to be managed and their rarity make that the actors are quickly overburdened and do not manage to face up efficiently to this type of event. Crisis management consists in dealing with the complexity and the interdependency of systems and especially with the combination of events [1]. Some researchers define approaches and techniques in order to define criteria to help assess the vulnerability of systems [2]. Others define organizations and communications guidelines in order to avoid vulnerability and deal with the crisis with minor consequences. The several steps of crisis to manage crisis can be summarized as [3]:

- Prevention: Preparation, planning, identification potential risks, definition of crisis cells and means definition of security tools and procedures, etc.

© IFIP International Federation for Information Processing 2019
Published by Springer Nature Switzerland AG 2019
E. Mercier-Laurent and D. Boulanger (Eds.): AI4KM 2017, IFIP AICT 571, pp. 99–112, 2019.
https://doi.org/10.1007/978-3-030-29904-0_8

- Formation: Trainings, evaluations, simulations, information and communication, etc.
- Problem solving: Crisis detection, alert, emergency plans and actions, activate protection actions, management actions, events, decisions and consequences, etc.
- Feedback: reporting, debriefing, brainstorming, risk evaluations, experience memorization, modifications procedures and means, etc.

Generally, there is a difference between real activity and procedures in crisis management situations. The events are different from each other and are strongly bound to exogenous parameters such as the political, economic, environmental situation, and societal. This paper shows how we tend to represent prediction of the consequences of a stress on crisis management. Firstly, we define a model that represents the impact of one actor to the situation considering the collaborative aspect of crisis and then we study stress consequences measurement.

2 Modelling Crisis Management

A crisis management is a collaborative situation, through which different dimensions must be studied: coordination [4], communication [5] and cooperative decision-making. In this type of situation there is an important relationship between individual actions and collaborative ones. Even actors follow training in order to face stress situations but the human condition (familial and life) and the disparity of situations in which the consequences (different type of victims (children, the elderly, etc.) push actors to lose control of situations. Note that crisis is defined as a situation out of control [1]. The question to answer is can we predict the consequence of a default to this type of situation? The aim of our work is to show a simulation of this prediction to actors as formation. For that, a model of the interaction between individual and team actions is defined. In this model, we mix systematic and collaboration models.

2.1 Crisis Definition and Crisis Management

The crisis is an unstable and dangerous situation affecting individual, group, community and the whole society. It generated a collective stress [6]. It is an exceptional situation. One of the definitions of crisis is: "a serious threat to the basic structures the fundamental values and, norms which under time pressure and, highly uncertain circumstances necessitates making a critical decision" [6]. Many types of crisis exist, as political, the contaminated blood crisis [7]; economic and financial, the Enron financial scandals [8]; technological, Challenger [9]; environmental crisis, Bhopal [10], Chernobyl [11] and, Exxon Valdez [12]. Crisis can have international, domestic and, local dimensions. A crisis request an organization to manage it and, to make pertinent decisions with the aim to request from this situation or to reduce its effect in a short time with minimal damage.

2.2   Systemic Modeling

Systemic or system science present a system as a complex interrelation between: structure and activity and evolution [13, 14]. This system has a finality and deals with the environment (see Fig. 1) through time and space.

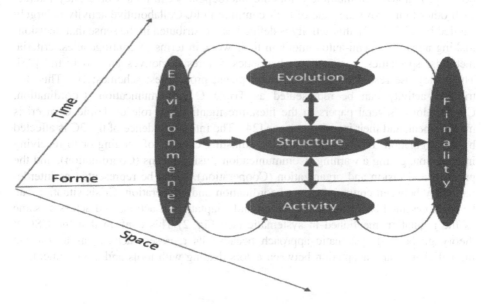

Fig. 1. Systemic model

The system has to regulate its operation facing variations. This phenomenon is called regulation. In fact, the system deals with variation by changing its composition and its state by losing members, adaptation and evolution of the structure and the activity [15, 16]. Stress and anxiety of an actor can be considered as a variation of the environment. We try to simulate in our work how the system can change in order to absorb this variation. Prediction techniques [17, 18] are generally used in order to simulate this change. Prediction algorithm is generally based on a nominal functioning model of the system. Based on that, several studies propose simulation of behaviors in crisis management like people behavior facing a problem [19] or actors in crisis [20]. But, as we note above, crisis in defined as the situation out of control. So, nominal function modelling is not possible. Only procedures and rules can be considered as a nominal situation. But, we know the reality is away from procedures especially in stress situations. Some work in prediction use Knowledge engineering and Case based reasoning in order to define a prediction system based on the experience of the use of components in industry [21]. So, we try to use this type of system but in collaborative situation.

2.3   Collaborative Situation Modeling

During a crisis management, the actors come from different organizations. They work, communicate, cooperate, coordinate and, exchange their own experiences. Their main common objective is how to deal with the crisis for reducing its effect? In this relationship, is noted that multiple actors are interdependent in their work. They interact each other to improve the state of their common field. Collaborative activity is largely studied in CSCW [22], this activity is defined as: "distributed in the sense that decision-making agents are semi-autonomous in their work in terms of contingencies, criteria, methods, specialties, perspectives, heuristics, interests, motives and so forth" [23]. Thus, they use resources like computers; plans; procedures; schemes; etc. This distributed activity can be represented as Triple C (Communication, Coordination, Cooperation). Several papers in the literature mention the role of Triple C in crisis management, and their interdependence [24]. The interdependence of the 3C is affected by the regulation. Indeed, the regulation adjusting consists of sending or to receiving information, giving a warning (Communication); using means (Coordination); and the procedure, decision and organization (Cooperation). It can be represented as interdependency between communication, coordination and cooperation. Crisis situation can be so represented as a constant evolution and adaptation of actions and actors as same as the regulation mentioned in systematic (see Fig. 2) This confirm that the CSCW theory go beyond systematic approach because its represent activity as a constant mutual change and adaptation between actors dealing with tools and environment.

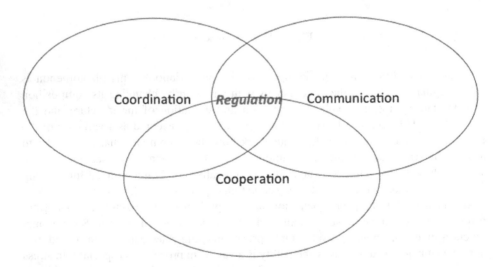

Fig. 2. Collaborative activity

2.4   Collaborative Crisis Management Modeling

As we noted above, crisis management is close to a chaotic situation then controlled one. It depends on different factors like situation misunderstanding; previous experience missing; actors stress, political and economic environment, etc. The crisis can be so represented as relations between event and states respecting this dynamicity [4] So, to represent real activities, we define crisis situations as several states evolving through time and space. Each state can be defined as event/consequences [4].

- Actor/role: is the concerned person or unit in each system state (crisis stage).
- Time: is the moment to do an action by the concerned actor according to place's type.
- Place: is the place concerned by the state.
- Data: is the available data for concerned actors in each moment, this piece of information is related to the characteristics of crisis situations, localization, weather and victims.
- Event: can be an action done by an actor or information related to a new environment element.

Actions can concern communication, coordination and cooperation. State can generate events and events can modify states (see Fig. 3). Five crisis management efforts are defined [1]:

1. Strategic efforts;
2. Technical and structural efforts;
3. Efforts in evaluation and diagnosis;
4. Communication efforts;
5. Psychological and cultural efforts.

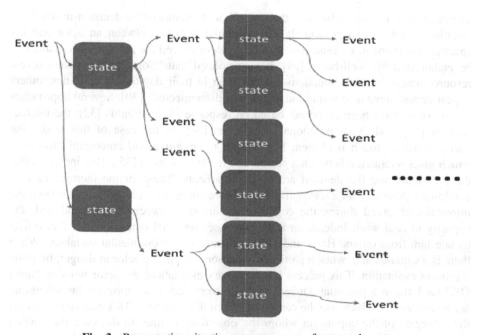

Fig. 3. Representing situation as a sequence of state and event

Stress is an important element to consider related to the psychological and cultural efforts. Stress is considered as variations in this environment. We present in the following this notion and how we aim at measuring its consequences as new events in a situation.

2.5   Using Experience Feedback in Crisis Management

In the daily life and, for any problem or situation, experience feedback is used. Yet, knowledge management approaches define some techniques to promote learning from experience feedback. So Foguem et al. present experience feedback as a "process of knowledge capitalization and exploitation mainly aimed at transforming understanding gained by experience into knowledge." [25]. This process shows five distinguished information: events, context, analysis, solutions and lessons learned. The literature on this domain has highlighted several tools to help companies and organizations, to avoid past mistakes and, to benefit from all the knowledge and the know-how used [4, 26–28]. By including experience feedback on technical and organizational means, actors can learn how to face stress in crisis management. Then, an actor or a group of actors can adjust its approaches; policies; procedures; methods; models and its organization, guided by previous experiences, to try to obtain as possible as a nominal situation

3   Stress

3.1   Stress and the Stress Indicators

The stress is an important factor in the success or the failure of the decision-making in a situation of crisis management. It is a particular relation between an actor and his specific environment. Its evaluation can be weak or exceed the actor resources and can be endangered his well-being [29]. It was noticed that "Some policymakers reveal resourcefulness in crisis situations seldom seen in their day-to-day activities; others appear erratic, devoid of sound judgment, and disconnected" [30]. Several approaches for the stress have been proposed, based on response [31]; stimulus [32]; the interactionism [33]; and the transactional approaches [34]. In the case of this study, the transactional approach is chosen. It is related to cognitive and emotional processes, which gives interaction between a person and his environment [35]. This indicates that the individual and the demand are two components. Those define themselves in a continuous process with a retroactive loop. More concretely, the stress result from the imbalance observed during the cognitive evaluation between the demand and, the capacity to deal with. Indeed, an actor possesses personal characteristics that differentiate him from others. He is under the influence of environmental variables. When there is a stimulus and, when a particular situation can put the actor in danger, he starts a process evaluation. This process has a primary evaluation, the actor wonder, "am I OK? Or I am in a potential danger" and, the secondary evaluation begins where the actor wonders by which way he can go out from this situation. This evaluation orients the strategies of the coping, in whom the objective is either to decrease the tension resulting from the situation, or to modify the situation [36]. [29] defined the coping as "the overall cognitive and behavioral efforts, continuously changing, deployed by an actor for managing specific internal and/or external requirements, which are evaluated as consuming or exceeding his resource". There are different studies that propose training and mental preparation methods to help actors to face the stress in crisis management [1, 37]. This paper focus on the impact of stress on decision-making in order to promote learning from fails and guides based on experience feedback.

3.2   The Stress Impact on a Crisis

Boswel et al. present four classes of indicators that influence stress conditions [35]:

- Task conditions: workload, etc.
- Relational conditions: conflict, harassment, etc.
- Job conditions: Mobility, no promotion, etc.
- Interaction private/profession: husband, children, family, etc.

Different observable indicators of the stress are considered in psychology as manifestations of stress. Some of these are mainly noted:

1. Speech rhythm [38, 39], repetition of expressions and words [40, 41], Using specific words [39, 40, 42, 43], etc.
2. Super activity, inadequate movement [44, 45], etc.
3. Silence [46].
4. Ambivalence, self-confidence [41, 46, 47].
5. Hostility and aggression [48].
6. Inappropriate behavior and actions [49, 50].

Some indicators that influence decision-making can be:

(a) Situation and context simplification [51, 52].
(b) Fixation on one possibility without any flexibility and alternatives [51, 53–55].
(c) Consulting several opinions without concluding on a decision [56, 57].
(d) Imposing a decision without measuring the impact and the consequences [56, 58].
(e) Missing decision-making and actions [56, 59].

For our work, we select some of these indicators that can be measured directly when actors deal with crisis. Indicators must be measurable without perturbing actions realizations and decision-making. So, stress manifestations as:

I. Super activity and imposing decision without considering the impact.
II. Silence, missing decision and actions.
III. Speech rhythm, aggression and conflict of opinions and decisions.
IV. Simplification of the situation and inadequate means and actions.

It is noted that different studies propose formation and mental preparation methods to help actors to face stress and anxiety in crisis management [37].

3.3   Using Feedback in Stress Situation

A crisis is by definition a stressed situation, outside of control. Therefore, stress is an important element to take into account when dealing with this type of situation. For instance, different manifestations of the stress like silence or aggression are present. In addition, impacts like simplification of the situation or consulting several opinions without concluding on a decision is noted. These impacts influence the decision-making. Related to each act and decision, stress can be increased or be reduced depending on the result of the decision and, in the state of actors. Here, the negative feedback comes into.

4   Example of Stress Impact in Crisis Situation

A real case study in a situation of crisis management. The author's observation can reveal some aspects of the impact of the stress during this event. It also provides, a timeline for actors reaction with a general view on errors committed, means used, the places where the event was reported and, different information and data known. For this, a retired officer of the Algerian Army has been interviewed (as an expert) about one of crisis situations he dealt with.

4.1   Case Description

A lieutenant of Algerian Army explains, in this case, his experience about a terrorist attack on two villages "Ramkaa and Had El Chekala", in the Algerian mountain. In fact, the army had to deal with a group of terrorists in the area. The tactical command post was installed near the mountain, in order to prepare their track. In the morning (6 h AM) of a day in February, some soldiers had been awake by a young man running to the camp and crying: "They killed them, they killed them." Soldiers tried to calm the young man and conducted him to the nursery. The crowd woke colonel and lieutenant. The young man explained then that the terrorists were killed all people in his village. Colonel asked the lieutenant to prepare three cars, and they directly went to villages with only simple guns. They drove on a winding road. Terrorist cloud is everywhere and could be attacking them. Arriving at the village, they discover horrible landscape, "everywhere dead bodies, disembowelled women, blood, etc." They were shocked and did not believe their eyes. One of the Chief starts to talk nonsense words. Soldiers removed his weapon, they were afraid about his safety. The Colonel decided then to visit the nearby village with the lieutenant and some soldiers. They discovered the same horrible situations, adding that, the school was burned with the nursery and the post-office. The colonel sat on the ground without moving. Soldiers and Lieutenant did not have any idea on how to react and what to do. Their radio did not work. There was no network. They stayed in this state more than one hour and a half. Then, other soldiers arrived at the base of ambulances and radio-communication post. Because they guess that their colleagues needed help after two hours of silence. After that, the colonel recovered his senses and called the government crisis cells. He called the tactical command post to send him fire fighters and medical emergency resources. It was about

10 h AM. Crisis Cells were installed at Ramkaa village. Dead Bodies were gathered. They discovered some survivals. They received first aid on site. Helicopters arrived and first evacuations started at 1 PM.

4.2   Analyzing the Stress Impact

The case analysis shows us some impact of the stress (see Fig. 4): (I) Imposing a decision without measuring the impact and the consequences: The colonel took three vehicles with simple guns and went to the village. He decided then to visit the nearby village with the lieutenant and some soldiers; (II) Repetition of expressions and words: One of the Chiefs started spelling nonsense words; (III) Silence, missing decision and actions: The colonel sat on the ground without moving. Soldiers and Lieutenant did not have any idea on how to react and what to do. (IV) Simplification of the situation and inadequate means and actions: With simple guns, they went to villages. Their radio did not work. There was no network. The impact of this stress during this situation is: time-lost; wounded died (waiting from 6 h AM to 1 h PM); the first soldiers can be attacked and killed by terrorists on the road and in the villages; no communications between operational and tactical teams. This analysis, show us, how the stress can cause considerable damage during a crisis situation. After analyzing the same case by using experience feedback different regulation actions can be identified.

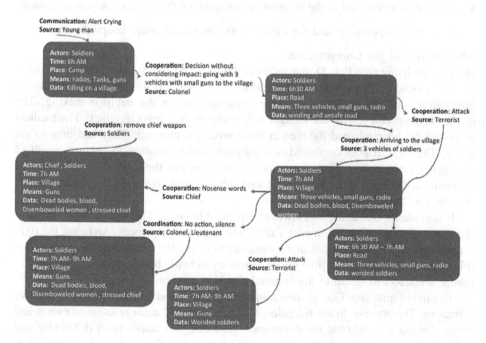

Fig. 4. Case modelling

4.3   Representing the Same Situation with Feedback Experience

After analyzing the same case using experience feedback and in an implicit manner the negative feedback, different regulation actions can be identified.

The Correct Case Description
The corrected description start when the young man gives the alert. At this moment, the Colonel will give the order to:

- A Reconnaissance Unit, accompanied by mine sweepers experts, got ready to go to see what happened?
- The Medical units got ready for a possible intervention in villages (field hospital, ambulances, helicopters of evacuation...).
- The hospitals around the city activated their plans of reception of the wounded victims.

Half an hour after, the unit of reconnaissance was ready and moved toward villages. On the road, this unity had the capability to counter a terrorist attack. Once there, the head of unity confirms the information to the Colonel and begins to secure villages to try to help survivors. The colonel at this moment will give:

- Order to the medical units to move to the village to be able to save lives and evacuate the wounded victims.
- Adapt its general staff to the situation to become a cell of emergency management.

At 9:00 am operations and the evacuations towards different hospitals began.

The Analyze of the Correct Case
For this modeling (see Fig. 5), the authors take back the stress impact model by using the same concept event/state. In this model, there was no time lost or moments of fluctuations due to uncertainties in the behavior and in the decision-making. The reconnaissance unit sent to the villages was ready for any terrorist attack. The medical units and the hospitals had the alert at the convenient moment. They had time to get ready. The tactical post command was adapted to the situation to become a cell of emergency management. The most important of all is that the Colonel makes the right decisions at the right time. He did not lose time to save lives. He also preserved his security and the security of his soldiers.

It is evidence that stress will always be present in crisis. The aim of this study is to show at each step: the stress impact actions and, their consequences. And also, the right actions and their consequences in the situation of crisis. By combining the two models (Figs. 4 and 5) and learning from errors, actors try to avoid bad decisions. These should ensure the actors to return to the nominal situation as soon as possible.

The next figure (see Fig. 6) shows an example of one state/event and compare two situations. The process, in the red color, represents the bad actor reaction to events and states. Taking into account the experience feedback, the actors react differently and make the best decisions, which will be saved a substantial time and maybe human lives (process in green). This view of these different situations concerns only the vision of the team of the tactical headquarters and the military engaged in this situation. This type of representation can help to apply prediction algorithms in order to propose a

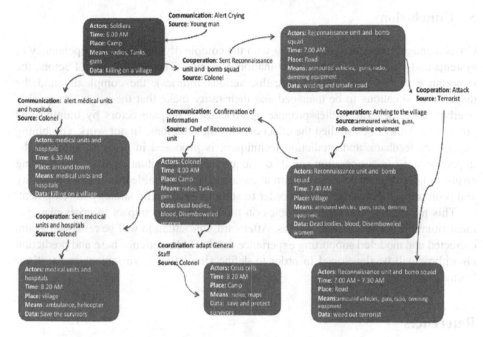

Fig. 5. Case modeling with feedback experience

simulation of stressful situations in a learning space. Before presenting our state prediction approach, let us first compare some prediction techniques.

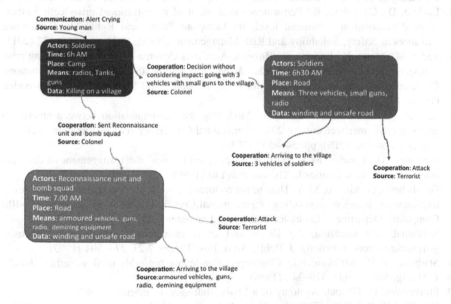

Fig. 6. Case modeling with and without feedback experience (Color figure online)

5 Conclusion

Crisis management consists in dealing with the complexity and the interdependency of systems and especially with the combination of events. The multiplicity of actors, the importance of the consequences (deaths, serious injuries), the complexity and the disparity of situations to be managed and their rarity make that the actors are quickly overburdened. Several studies propose approaches to prepare actors by training and prevention. Other ones studied the effect of stress in situations. In our work, combining experience feedback and prediction techniques, is proposed in order to simulate the impact of stress in cooperation and its consequences on the situation state. By showing errors and correctness actions, we aim at engaging operational learning close to reality and promoting cognitive chocks in order to stimulate reasoning strategy development.

This paper presents our first studies on modelling stress impact in crisis management situations for prediction systems. Afterward, this situation will be reviewed again, corrected and modeled supporting experience feedback. Experience base and prediction algorithms will be developed in order to define simulation environment and test our learning hypothesis.

References

1. Pauchant, T.C., Mitroff, I.I., Lagadec, P.: Toward a systemic crisis management strategy: learning from the best examples in the US, Canada and France. Ind. Cris. Q. 5(3), 209–232 (1991)
2. Swartout, W., et al.: Toward the holodeck: integrating graphics, sound, character and story. University of Southern California Marina del Rey CA Inst for Creative Technologies (2006)
3. Lachtar, D., Garbolino, E.: Performance evaluation of organizational crisis cell: methodological proposal at communal level. In: European Safety and Reliability Conference: Advances in Safety, Reliability and Risk Management, ESREL 2011, pp. 165–172 (2011)
4. Sediri, M., Matta, N., Loriette, S., Hugerot, A.: Crisis clever, a system for supporting crisis managers. In: Proceedings of IEEE, ACM, Proceeding ISCRAM, 10th International Conference on Information Systems for Crisis Response and Management, Baden-Baden, Germany (2013)
5. Saoutal, A., Cahier, J.-P., Matta, N.: Modelling the communication between emergency actors in crisis management. In: 2014 International Conference on Collaboration Technologies and Systems (CTS), pp. 545–552 (2014)
6. Rosenthal, U., Charles, M.T., Hart, P.: Coping with crises: the management of disasters, riots, and terrorism. Charles C Thomas Pub Ltd (1989)
7. De Michelis, G., Grasso, M.A.: How to put cooperative work in context: analysis and design requirements. Issues of Supporting Organizational Context in CSCW Systems, pp. 73–100. Computing Department, Lancaster University, Lancaster (1993)
8. Rosenthal, U., Kouzmin, A.: Crises and crisis management: toward comprehensive government decision-making. J. Public Adm. Res. Theory 7(2), 277–304 (1997)
9. Starbuck, W.H., Milliken, F.J.: Challenger: fine-tuning the odds until something breaks. J. Manag. Stud. 25(4), 319–340 (1988)
10. Shrivastava, P.: Bhopal: Anatomy of a Crisis. Ballinger, Cambridge (1987)
11. Beck, U.: Risk Society: Towards a New Modernity, vol. 17. Sage, Thousand Oaks (1992)

12. Pauchant, T.C., Mitroff, I.I.: Transforming the Crisis-Prone Organization: Preventing Individual, Organizational, and Environmental Tragedies. Jossey-Bass, San Francisco (1992)
13. Le Moigne, J.L.: Modeling of complex systems. AFCET systems, headed by Bernard Paulré Collection, p. 24. Dunod, Paris (1990)
14. Bernard-Weil, E.: Systémique ago antagoniste. In: Systémique Théorie et Apllications, Lavoisier., pp. 46–62. Technique & Documentation - Lavoisier, Paris (1992)
15. Von Bertalanffy, L.: General system theory. New York **41973**(1968), 40 (1968)
16. Morin, E.: Method. Towards a study of humankind, vol. 1: The Nature of nature/Morin Edgar. Peter Lang, New York (1992)
17. Wiener, N., Masani, P.: The prediction theory of multivariate stochastic processes. Acta Math. **98**(1–4), 111–150 (1957)
18. Helson, H., Lowdenslager, D.: Prediction theory and Fourier series in several variables. Acta Math. **99**(1), 165–202 (1958)
19. Jaffrelot, M., Boet, S., Di Cioccio, A., Michinov, E., Chiniara, G.: Simulation et gestion de crise Simulation and crisis resource management. Réanimation **22**(6), 569–576 (2013)
20. Hinske, S., Langheinrich, M.: An infrastructure for interactive and playful learning in augmented toy environments. In: IEEE International Conference on Pervasive Computing and Communications, PerCom 2009, pp. 1–6 (2009)
21. Khelif, R., Chebel-Morello, B., Malinowski, S., Laajili, E., Fnaiech, F., Zerhouni, N.: Direct remaining useful life estimation based on support vector regression. IEEE Trans. Ind. Electron. **64**(3), 2276–2285 (2017)
22. Schmidt, K., Simonee, C.: Coordination mechanisms: towards a conceptual foundation of CSCW systems design. Comput. Support. Coop. Work **5**(2–3), 155–200 (1996)
23. Schmidt, K.: Cooperative work and its articulation: requirements for computer support. Trav. Hum. **57**(4), 345–366 (1994)
24. Martin, E., Nolte, I., Vitolo, E.: The Four Cs of disaster partnering: communication, cooperation, coordination and collaboration. Disasters **40**(4), 621–643 (2016)
25. Foguem, B.K., Coudert, T., Béler, C., Geneste, L.: Knowledge formalization in experience feedback processes: an ontology-based approach. Comput. Ind. **59**(7), 694–710 (2008)
26. Nonaka, I., Takeuchi, H.: The Knowledge-Creating Company: How Japanese Companies Create the Dynamics of Innovation. Oxford University Press, Oxford (1995)
27. Grundstein, M.: From capitalizing on company knowledge to knowledge management. Knowl. Manag. Class. Contemp. Work. **12**, 261–287 (2000)
28. Dieng-Kuntz, R., Matta, N.: Knowledge Management and Organizational Memories. Springer, New York (2002). https://doi.org/10.1007/978-1-4615-0947-9
29. Lazarus, R.S., Folkman, S.: Stress, Appraisal, and Coping. Springer, Heidelberg (1984)
30. Hermann, M.G.: Indicators of stress in policymakers during foreign policy crises. Polit. Psychol. **1**(1), 27–46 (1979)
31. Selye, H.: Stress Without Distress, pp. 26–39. New York (1974)
32. Hobfoll, S.E.: Conservation of resources: a new attempt at conceptualizing stress. Am. Psychol. **44**(3), 513 (1989)
33. Jones, F., Bright, J., Clow, A.: Stress: Myth. Theory and Research. Pearson Education, New York (2001)
34. Cox, T., Griffiths, A., Rial-González, E.: Research on Work-Related Stress. European Communities (2000)
35. Boswell, W.R., Olson-Buchanan, J.B., LePine, M.A.: Relations between stress and work outcomes: the role of felt challenge, job control, and psychological strain. J. Vocat. Behav. **64**(1), 165–181 (2004)
36. Van Damme, S., Crombez, G., Eccleston, C.: Coping with pain: a motivational perspective. Pain **139**(1), 1–4 (2008)

37. Ducrocq, F., Vaiva, G., Cottencin, O., Molenda, S., Bailly, D.: Post-traumatic stress, post-traumatic depression and major depressive episode: literature. Encephale **27**(2), 159–168 (2000)

38. Kanfer, F.H.: Verbal rate, content and adjustment ratlngs in experimentally structured interviews. I. abnorm. soc. Psychol **58**, 402 (1959)

39. Siegman, A.W., Pope, B.: Studies in Dyadic Communication. Elsevier, Amsterdam (2016)

40. Kasl, S.V., Mahl, G.F.: The relationship of disturbances and hesitations in spontaneous speech to anxiety. J. Pers. Soc. Psychol. **1**(5), 425–433 (1965)

41. Osgood, C.E., Walker, E.G.: Motivation and language behavior: a content analysis of suicide notes. J. Abnorm. Soc. Psychol. **59**(1), 58 (1959)

42. Lalljee, M., Cook, M.: Uncertainty in first encounters. J. Pers. Soc. Psychol. **26**(1), 137 (1973)

43. Maclay, H., Osgood, C.E.: Hesitation phenomena in spontaneous English speech. Word **15**(1), 19–44 (1959)

44. Dittmann, A.T.: The relationship between body movements and moods in interviews. J. Consult. Psychol. **26**(5), 480 (1962)

45. Mehrabian, A., Ksionzky, S.: Categories of social behavior. Comp. Group Stud. **3**(4), 425–436 (1972)

46. Aronson, H., Weintraub, W.: Personal adaptation as reflected in verbal behavior. In: Studies in Dyadic Communication, pp. 265–278. Pergamon Press, New York (1972)

47. Eichler, M.: The application of verbal behavior analysis to the study of psychological defense mechanisms: speech patterns associated with sociopathic behavior. J. Nerv. Ment. Dis. **141**(6), 658–663 (1965)

48. Gottschalk, L.A., Winget, C.M., Gleser, G.C., Springer, K.J.: The measurement of emotional changes during a psychiatric interview: a working model toward quantifying the psychoanalytic concept of affect. In: Gottschalk, L.A., Auerbach, A.H. (eds.) Methods of Research in Psychotherapy, pp. 93–126. Springer, Boston (1966). https://doi.org/10.1007/978-1-4684-6045-2

49. Mehrabian, A.: Relationship of attitude to seated posture, orientation, and distance. J. Pers. Soc. Psychol. **10**(1), 26 (1968)

50. Mehrabian, A.: Inference of attitudes from the posture, orientation, and distance of a communicator. J. Consult. Clin. Psychol. **32**(3), 296 (1968)

51. Holsti, O.R., Brody, R.A., North, R.C.: Measuring affect and action in inter national reaction models empirical materials from the 1962 cuban crisis. J. Peace Res. **1**(3–4), 170–189 (1964)

52. Lazarus, R.S, Opton Jr, E.M., Spielberger, C.D.: The study of psychological stress: a summary of theoretical formulations and experimental findings. In: Anxiety and Behavior, vol. 1 (1966)

53. Berkowitz, L.: Aggression: A social psychological analysis (1962)

54. De Rivera, J.: The Psychological Dimension of Foreign Policy. CE Merrill Pub. Co. (1968)

55. Rosenblatt, P.C.: Origins and effects of group ethnocentrism and nationalism. J. Conflict Resolut. **8**(2), 131–146 (1964)

56. Holsti, O.R.: Crisis Escalation War. McGill-Queen's Press-MQUP (1972)

57. Edwards, J.R., Cooper, C.L.: Research in stress, coping, and health: theoretical and methodological issues. Psychol. Med. **18**(1), 15–20 (1988)

58. Korchin, S.J.: Anxiety and cognition. Cogn. Theory, Res. promise, ed. E. Scheerer. Harper Row.[PFG] (1964)

59. Schlenker, B.R., Miller, R.S.: Egocentrism in groups: self-serving biases or logical information processing? J. Pers. Soc. Psychol. **35**(10), 755 (1977)

Detecting Influencial Users in Social Networks: Analysing Graph-Based and Linguistic Perspectives

Kévin Deturck[1,2], Namrata Patel[1,3(✉)], Pierre-Alain Avouac[1],
Cédric Lopez[1,4], Damien Nouvel[2], Ioannis Partalas[1,5],
and Frédérique Segond[1,2]

[1] Viseo, Grenoble, France
{kevin.deturck,namrata.patel,pierre-alain.avouac,
cedric.lopez,ioannis.partalas,
frederique.segond}@viseo.com
[2] INaLCO-ERTIM, Paris, France
{kevin.deturck,damien.nouvel,
frederique.segond}@inalco.fr
[3] Université Paul Valéry, Montpellier, France
Namrata.Patel@univ-montp3.fr
[4] Emvista, Montpellier, France
cedric.lopez@emvista.com
[5] Expedia, Lausanne, Switzerland
ioannis.partalas@gmail.com

Abstract. There has been increasing interest in the artificial intelligence community for influencer detection in recent years for its utility in singling out pertinent users within a large network of social media users. This could be useful, for example in commercial campaigns, to promote a product or a brand to a relevant target set of users. This task is performed either by analysing the graph-based representation of user interactions in a social network or by measuring the impact of the linguistic content of user messages in online discussions. We performed independent studies for each of these methods in the present paper with a hybridisation perspective. In the first study, we extract structural information to highlight influence among interaction networks. In the second, we identify linguistic features of influential behaviours. We then compute a score of user influence using centrality measures with the structural information for the former and a machine learning approach based on the relevant linguistic features for the latter.

Keywords: Influence · Social media · Linguistics · Centrality

1 Introduction

An influencer can be characterised as a person that has the power to affect people, actions or events. In recent years, There has been increasing interest in the artificial intelligence (AI) community for influencer detection in recent years for its utility in singling out pertinent users within a large network of social media users. Such

© IFIP International Federation for Information Processing 2019
Published by Springer Nature Switzerland AG 2019
E. Mercier-Laurent and D. Boulanger (Eds.): AI4KM 2017, IFIP AICT 571, pp. 113–131, 2019.
https://doi.org/10.1007/978-3-030-29904-0_9

information is crucial in many research studies such as in sociology and information management domains.

Additionally, with the frenetic growth of available data in social media, being able to analyse and detect influential users becomes crucial as they are susceptible to express their ideas with a greater impact than other individuals. This could be useful, for example in commercial campaigns, to promote a product or a brand to a relevant target set of users and maximise their spread [1].

Influencer detection is usually performed by analysing a graph-based representation of user interactions in a social network. In this context, studies using graph theory leverage the structural information in these graphs to identify the most important nodes in a network [2, 3].

Following another line of thought, a recent development in the task has been to analyse the textual content of the messages posted by the users to identify character-istics of communication for influence detection [4, 5].

We further explore both aspects in this paper with two independent studies, each generating the following specific contexts, based on their respective requirements: (1) a social network featuring various interaction types for graph analysis [24] and (2) a forum that provides written posts as the only means of expression, for linguistic analysis. These two studies respectively allow us to (1) observe the interaction types and users' positions in graphs that highlight influential users and (2) address the influence of the linguistic content of user's messages.

Regarding graph analysis, we compare various interaction types in their capacity to denote influence between users. We build the graph from selected interactions to get their structure in a formal way. From this structure, we analyse users' positions and determine those that reflect influence among interactions. We use centrality measures considering a central position in interaction networks as an indicator of influence.

In developing our linguistic approach, we compare linguistic criteria (such as a user's argumentation, agreement/disagreement between users) with classical numerical criteria (number of answers, message size, number of relations, etc.). The former is extracted using a symbolic approach based on a set of linguistic rules while the latter is extracted from available metadata on the messages. This information is then integrated into an automatic learning system. The resulting system is thus a "doubly hybrid" system, since it is based on symbolic and statistical methods on the one hand, and information structure and textual content on the other. To facilitate the interpretation of results and to better represent the different aspects addressed in our approach, we complete our system with an interface for knowledge visualisation.

The rest of the article is organised as follows. In Sect. 2 we provide a general overview of existing techniques in influence detection within social media, situating our approaches in their scientific context. We then describe our approaches in Sect. 3 and follow it up with their respective evaluations in Sect. 4.

2   Related Work

With the growing number of users interacting through social media and the increasing amounts of available data for research, social media information has become a con-siderable source for user behaviour analysis. For influence detection, in particular, social media contains a significant amount of information which can be exploited at the level of (1) user interactions and (2) message content. This has led to two main lines of work.

2.1 Influencer Detection by Social Network Analysis (SNA)

The first axis of work in this domain is primarily based on graph theory, where influential behaviour is computed by analysing the structural information of user interactions contained within a given sample of a social network. SNA meets graph theory as user interactions are formally represented in a graph with users as vertices and interactions as edges. Among the different types of social media, including forums, blogs and social networks, the latter are commonly studied for graph analysis as it offers more diverse user interactions. For example, Twitter provides "follow", "like" and "reply" while forums or blogs only provide "reply" and "quote" as interactions.

[6] introduces the idea that there is a connection between an individual's central position among the interactions of a group and their influence within the same group. [7] formalises the centrality intuition and proposes a first set of graph centrality measures, including *degree*, *proximity* and *betweenness* measures. Centrality measures compute a centrality score for each vertex in a graph according to a specific edge configuration. For example, the *degree* measure uses the number of direct edges from a vertex while *proximity* measures the average path length (number of edges) from one vertex to others. The centrality score of a vertex indicates its influence value in a graph. With the growing popularity of web pages, a new centrality measure was defined, PageRank [3], to take into account hyperlinks between pages. Applying different centrality measures on social graphs which represent different interaction types provides various aspects of influence measurement. [8] applies a proximity measure on scientific citation networks to measure the influence of researchers. [9] highlights the importance of the community to analyse centrality. Authors claim that users of a social network tend to communicate with users of a same group, for example regarding a specific topic. They detect communities in a social network sample before computing users' influence value in each community. [10] fine-tunes the selection of interactions distinguishing user-level from content-level interactions in a multilayer adaptation of PageRank.

Some works defined influencers according to their capacity to motivate individuals towards an action or a message, thus detecting them by analysing the propagation of interactions. In a graph, an influential vertex could replicate its behaviour in a fast and deep way. This vision relates to the key problem of influence maximisation through a network. [11] predicts the interaction dynamics from a graph node to estimate its influence. [12] analyses information spread to detect influencers. [13] associates influencers with users who are able to maximise their opinion through a network.

2.2 Influencer Detection by Linguistic Analysis

The second axis of work delves into the semantic aspects of the user messages, identifying influential behaviour through linguistic markers. Recent research in this category aims at identifying characteristics of influential behaviour through linguistic markers present within the messages. [14] focuses on the opinions expressed in messages to follow influential trends. [15] and [5] describe several behavioural features such as persuasion, agreement/disagreement, dialog patterns and sentiments which characterise influence and propose a machine learning approach to detect influential users. [16] identifies influencers by a specific language use including emotion lexicon and personal pronouns to establish a proximity with their audience, thus facilitating the message transmission.

As we mentioned the importance of community in SNA state-of-the-art, linguistic analysis helps with finding communities regarding a topic. [17] drives influence detection according to topic detection in users' messages.

This line of work provides promising results in influence detection, given the depth of scrutiny involved in the analysis of influential behaviour that we can relate to particular effects for the audience like opinion change.

2.3   Influencer Detection by Hybridisation

The challenge of combining both axes of research is relatively less explored. [18] biases PageRank towards certain users according to a specific topic. More recently, [19] proposed a supervised random walk approach towards topic-sensitive influential nodes. As can be seen, the message content is exploited here only in terms of the topic. Taking into account the second line of research, this challenge can be addressed by focussing on the semantic aspects of the message content.

In the aim of combining these two lines of research, as a first step, we independently explore each in their own context. These can then be capitalised upon with a hybridisation perspective. Focusing on the semantic aspects of message content, we develop a linguistic rule-based reasoning engine to identify linguistic markers for influential behaviour in a corpus of forum discussions. As for the SNA approach, we propose an exploration of some centrality measures applied on a manually annotated Twitter[1] dataset in order to determine those centrality measures and Twitter interactions that are relevant to influence detection.

Performing these studies independently allows us to analyse them respectively in favourable conditions, as each of them has specific requirements that are not compatible with the other. For example, graph-based studies require complex interactions which forums cannot provide and linguistic studies require substantial textual content which Twitter cannot provide.

3   Methodology

We propose an exploration of the two main ways to detect influencers. (1) Linguistic analysis and (2) centrality computation are tested separately on specific datasets that conform to the respective requirements of the two types of analysis: (1) a forum that allows long messages for linguistic analysis and (2) Twitter featuring different

---

[1] http://www.twitter.com.

interaction types for SNA. Both experiments can be broken down into the four following phases:

1. Corpus construction from social-media source
2. Selection of linguistic and structural features
3. System design
4. Visualisation

We now describe each work in further details.

3.1 Corpus Construction

Forum Dataset

The data used to elaborate the influencer detection algorithm comes from an English
forum in the domain of cosmetics[2] which contains different discussions about makeup
products, beauty tips, *etc*. We have scraped more than 5,000 threads from this forum
and randomly divided the corpus in three different groups. The first group,
RuleDevelopment, consists of 1000 threads reserved for analysis and to develop linguistic rules; the second group, *TrainingSet*, also consists of 1,000 threads and serves
as training data for the machine learning module; the third group, *TestSet*, consists of
the rest of the threads (3,000) and is used to evaluate our approach. Each of the 18,085
messages within the second group (dedicated to training the machine learning model
and 1027 messages within the third group was manually annotated to reflect a boolean
value per message: whether or not the message is influential.

We consider as influential a message that contains specific linguistic features reflecting
influential behaviour (further described in Sect. 3.2). We therefore defined an annotation guide specifying how an annotator may recognize these features. For example,
the following message shows that its author has been *argumentative*. "What is the look
for this season? Is the dewy face in or a matte one? I see some stars with make up
where their face is dewy and *it looks nice, but I can't stand doing that. I have to make
my face matte or otherwise I feel shiny and oily*."

Twitter Dataset

As a ground-truth, we chose a dataset made for RepLab 2014 [20]. This lab included a
task that consisted in ranking Twitter users according to their real-world influence. The
dataset contains more than 7,000 accounts split according to their domain: bank,
automotive and others. Accounts were binary annotated depending on whether they
were real-world influencers or not by the online reputation experts Llorente & Cuenca[3].
The dataset contains in average 1/3 of influencers.

---

[2] We dissimulate the name of the forum for reasons of confidentiality.

[3] www.llorenteycuenca.com/en/.

3.2 Features

In Sect. 1, we defined influence as a power, that leads us to characterise influencers according to the resources and effects of this power. We look for these two aspects analysing interaction content and structure.

Features from the Forum Dataset

During this phase, the corpus is analysed to identify criteria related to influential behaviour, as cited in the section above and described in Table 1. We distinguish between "linguistic" and "non-linguistic" criteria to separate the linguistic information from the structural one. The former is extracted on the basis of a set of linguistic rules. The latter is computed using count functions or by determining a boolean value.

To extract the linguistic features, we develop a separate module for each type of feature. We have 3 modules: (1) Writing style, (2) Argumentation and (3) Agreement/Disagreement. Each of these modules consists of the linguistic rules specific to the corresponding linguistic feature, developed by analysing the portion of the corpus kept aside for this purpose (*RuleDevelopment*). All the linguistic rules are based on a morphosyntactic analysis performed by the Eloquant Semantic Solutions[4] parser. We now detail each of these linguistic modules.

Argumentation

To detect instances of argumentation within the messages, we base ourselves on the study described in [20]. An argument is defined as a set of propositions, each of them being a premise, with at most one being a conclusion.

Thus, we focus on the identification of messages that potentially contain premises and/or conclusions. For instance, "This product is not reliable and very expensive!" is a premise, and "Then I can't recommend buying it!" is a conclusion.

Writing Style

To extract features corresponding to "writing style", we exploit the way in which authors express their opinions. We detect four indicators of writing style.

- *Elongation*, e.g. "greeeeeeeeat"
- *Uppercase*, e.g. "I LOVE this product"
- *Exclamation/Interrogation*, e.g. "You should try it!!!!"
- *Advising*, e.g. "You can buy this product"

Agreement/Disagreement

We develop the Agreement/Disagreement module on the basis of the following question: Does the author agree/disagree with previous author? For instance, in the following sentence: "I'm not going the same way as Mary", the system might be able to detect a disagreement.

All the rules developed for the different linguistic modules follow the same general pattern and are adapted according to the linguistic feature to be extracted. This pattern is described as:

---

[4] https://www.eloquant.com/en/semantic/explore-automatic-semantic-analysis.

Table 1. Description of the features extracted to be used in the machine learning model.

Category	Type of the features	Features	Output
Non-linguistic features	Position of the post in a thread	isFirstPost?	Boolean
Non-linguistic features	Position of the post in a thread	isSecondPost?	Boolean
Non-linguistic features	Position of the post in a thread	isPenultimateost?	Boolean
Non-linguistic features	Position of the post in a thread	isLatestPost?	Boolean
Non-linguistic features	Quantitative information	sizeOfMessages	Integer
Non-linguistic features	Dates	RegistrationDate	Date
Non-linguistic features	Location	Location of the user	String
Linguistic features	Writing style	Elongation	Boolean
Linguistic features	Writing style	Uppercase	Boolean
Linguistic features	Writing style	Exclamation	Boolean
Linguistic features	Writing style	Interrogation	Boolean
Linguistic features	Writing style	Advising	Boolean
Linguistic features	Argumentation	Nb of premises	Integer
Linguistic features	Argumentation	conclusion?	Boolean
Linguistic features	Argumentation	ArgumentInFirstSentence	Boolean
Linguistic features	Agreement/Disagreement	Agreement	Boolean
Linguistic features	Agreement/Disagreement	Disagreement	Boolean

1. *Construction of lexicons based on the state-of-the-art i.e.* detection of premises: "as shown by", "is implied by", "on the supposition that", "may be deduced from",...; Detection of conclusions: "concludes", "proves", "entails", "lead me to believe that", "bear out the point that", "it must be that",...
2. *Morphosyntactic analysis with Eloquant parser*: we use the lemma and the form in order to take into account variations such as "is implied by", "was implied by",...
3. *Application of rules* destined to detect whether a phrase from one of the lexicons (and all its variations) appears in a given message.

The messages are thus automatically annotated according to the different detected features. These then serve as input for the machine learning model that computes an influence score per message.

Features from the Twitter Dataset

As influence needs interactions (unidirectional actions from a user to another user), we focus on selecting Twitter interactions as features. We present Twitter interaction types in Table 2 excluding private message as, by definition, it is not accessible. We put in bold the types we finally selected. The principle of this selection was to work on interaction types that denote an influence on issuers from receivers. For each type, we analyse the engagement it implies for issuers towards receivers. *Follow* is the only interaction type that directly denotes an engagement at user-level. As influencers are basically users, we retain it. We decide to compare this user-level interaction type with one at content-level. Of the other three types, *answer* is the one that provides the least semantics by itself, requiring linguistic analysis; as this is not the point of the SNA exploration, we eliminated it. *Retweet* and *Like* have similar constitutions (cf. Table 2) and both indicate an interest from issuer for a content produced by receiver. However, we noticed that *retweet* is a stronger engagement as it affects a larger audience (cf. Table 2), we therefore retain it as a second feature.

Table 2. Twitter public interactions.

Nom	Source type	Target type	Main effect	Audience
Retweet	User	Tweet	Related tweet	As for source
Like	User	Tweet	Bookmark	As for source
Answer	Tweet	Tweet	Related tweet	Twitter
Following	User	User	Subscription	As for source

3.3   System Design

System Design for Linguistic Analysis: Machine Learning Model Generation
We presented in Sect. 3.2 the identification of linguistic and non-linguistic features to detect an influential behaviour in the forum dataset. During this phase, each message is described in terms of the features it contains. The entire dataset is therefore represented as a matrix: each line represents a message and each column represents a feature that it contains. Feature values for a given message are filled in on the basis of the annotations present within it.

This feature matrix is fed to the machine learning model in order to compute the final influence score per message. We chose to employ Random Forests (RF) as they are proven to be robust and state-of-the-art methods across several applications. Essentially, a random forest algorithm creates multiple decision trees by learning simple rules. A decision of membership is made according to prediction probabilities. Figure 1 presents a simple decision tree where the nodes in rectangles represent the leaf-level nodes and the prediction probability for a message to be influential is visually represented in burgundy.

The procedure described above is applied to each message in the corpus. Therefore, as output at this stage, we have an influence score per message which represents the probability of responding positively to the question "Is this message influential?". These influence scores are then aggregated to produce a final influence score per author. This aggregation is done by exploiting the structural information present in the network of user interactions (authors).

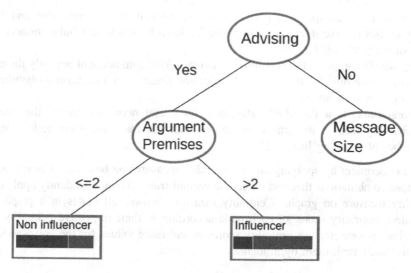

Fig. 1. A simple decision tree computed by our model.

Let $U = \{u_1, u_2, \ldots, u_n\}$ be the set of users in a social network and $S_u = \{s_1, s_2, \ldots, s_{K_u}\}$ be the set of scores for each post of user u, where $K_u =$ number of messages posted by u. Then we define the following normalised aggregated value as the final influence score for each user:

$$Inf(u) = \frac{\frac{1}{K_u} \sum_{i=1}^{K_u} s_i}{max_{u'} \sum_{j=1}^{K_{u'}} s_j \frac{1}{K_{u'}}} \tag{1}$$

Formalisation for Centrality Computation: Graph Construction and Centralities
As we detect influencers as particular Twitter users, we only build user graphs, even for *retweet* which is at content-level. In a graph, we represent both interactions described in Sect. 3.2 as orientated edges between users as nodes (from issuer to receiver). We build one graph per interaction type.

We distinguish two types of centrality: local, that only takes into account direct links from a node, and global, that uses the whole graph. We select six centrality measures from these two types because of their complementarity and popularity. Both constitute different influence models that we detail below.

- *Incoming degree*: directly uses the number of incoming links for a given node. It is a direct polarization towards a user [7].
- *Betweenness* and *Proximity*: compute the shortest paths between all nodes in a graph to respectively get how much a node is present on it and how distant a node is on average from other ones [7]. We did not get results for these measures because we obtained disconnected graphs on which we cannot compute shortest paths between all nodes. Nonetheless, we mention them because they still are part of our experiments.

- *Hits*: is more complex as it computes two mutual scores: authority and hub. Authorities receive interactions in particular from hubs whereas hubs connect to a lot of authorities [21].
- *PageRank*: computes the centrality of a node taking into account not only the edge configuration but also the weight of edges and nodes with a uniform probability to "jump" between nodes [3].
- *LeaderRank*: is a PageRank adaptation for social networks setting the "jump" probability from a uniform value to one that decreases for each node with its number of outgoing links [22].

We experiment by applying the six centrality measures on both interaction types to find those combinations that best reflect the ground-truth. We independently apply each centrality measure on graphs. Centrality measures browse all nodes in a graph and compute a centrality score for each node according to their respective centrality formalisation. We strictly use centrality scores as influence values for the corresponding users to finally rank them by influence.

3.4   Visualisation

For a comprehensive visualisation of influential users, we develop a knowledge visualisation module which describes (1) a graphical representation of the users ranked by influence, (2) the user interactions present in a given thread (3) the message threads annotated to highlight the detected linguistic features. The module is web-based to allow for straightforward accessibility.

Based on the linguistic analysis performed by the system under the hood, the module presents a special feature that offers the possibility of filtering of social users according to *key-terms* or *topics of interest*. This gives a fine-grained view on the set of influencers. The module also provides a global view of the detected influencers using different visualisation methods such as a bar chart or a bubble chart.

Figure 2 presents a screen of the visualization module where the top 20 users are ranked in a bar chart according to their score of influence. Figure 3 presents the interaction among users in a graph for a certain discussion. Users with higher score of influence are represented with bigger circles.

Apart from visualising the set of users, the module also offers a view of the message threads analysed to compute an influence score. The features used as input for the machine learning model are highlighted within the sentences to offer a contextual explanation of message content that is relevant to computing the final influence score.

The visualization module was actually made for a demonstration of the Soma project[5] which does not feature centrality computation to compute scores of influence. Pursuing our hybridisation perspective, we intend to extend the visualization module so that one can select the features used to compute users' influence score including their

---

[5] The linguistic study was a part of the SOMA Eurostars project (SOMA Eurostars program 9292/12/19892, http://www.somaproject.eu/) which concerns the enhancement of customer relationship management systems with social media analysis capabilities.

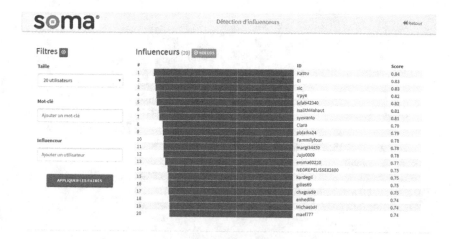

Fig. 2. Influencer ranking visualisation.

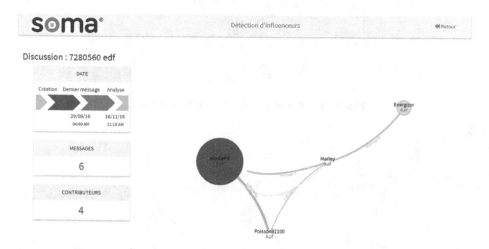

Fig. 3. The interaction graph of users throughout a discussion.

centrality score. Nonetheless, we save Twitter data in a Neo4j[6] database that offers a graph browser to visualize the information one requests. Figures 4 and 5 respectively present screenshots of follow and retweet graphs with yellow circles as user nodes and blue circles as tweet nodes. We can observe that these two graphs are more complex than the conversation one presented in Fig. 3 thus analysing their structure with centrality measures seems particularly relevant.

---

[6] https://neo4j.com.

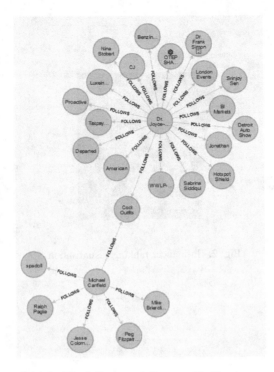

Fig. 4. The follow graph between Twitter users.

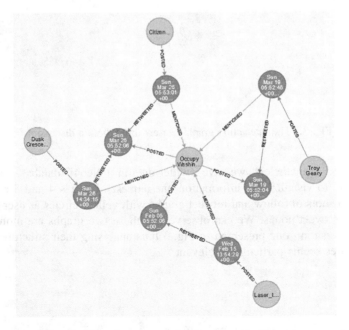

Fig. 5. The retweet graph between two Twitter users.

4 Evaluation

Our primary aim in evaluating our approach is to assess the relevance of including a linguistic analysis of message content in the detection of influencers. We therefore perform experiments that compare the performance of our developed system with and without the linguistic analysis. We also rank the influence criteria used as features in the ML model by order of importance to identify how linguistic features fare compared to the traditionally used numerical ones.

We evaluate the different combinations of centrality measures and interactions types by comparing user rankings they produce against the RepLab binary reference as an Information Retrieval (IR) task: best rankings must return the most of influencer users in higher positions. We now describe the experimental setup and the obtained results.

4.1 Experimental Setup

Linguistic Approach

To evaluate the proposed approach we used the corpus described in Sect. 3.1. During evaluation we omitted *RuleDevelopment*, the portion reserved to develop linguistic rules, to avoid any resulting bias. We first trained the ML model using the manually annotated TrainingSet, then tested the model on TestSet. Our selected ML model, Random Forests, also allowed the extraction of feature importance. This is particularly useful to evaluate the pertinence of the linguistic features used in computing an influence score.

To train the machine learning model we used RF for which we performed a random search coupled with 5-fold cross validation to tune its parameters: (1) number of trees tuned to the interval $\in$ [50, 500], (2) the depth $\in$ [2, 10] and (3) the information criterion $\in$ {*entropy, gini*}. We trained two versions of the model, with and without linguistic features in order to asses their relevance. The two models were optimized for ROC-AUC which is a measure of the probability that a positive instance will be ranked higher than a negative one.

Centrality Approach

Limited by Twitter API usage rates[7] for extracting interactions, we decided to sample the RepLab dataset at 50 users maintaining the original 1/3 influencer proportion for comparability purposes with the lab participant systems and filtering by bank domain to get a community-like representation.

Building one graph for each interaction type allows us to compare centrality measures among them. We extracted all *follow* relationships regarding our sample and represented it in a *follow graph*. Considering *retweet*, we selected the last ten tweets from each user's timeline and extracted the retweets in the limit of 100 imposed by Twitter API. To build a user graph while *retweet* is a content-level interaction, we represented as nodes the retweet authors instead of the retweets itself, assigning a

---

[7] https://developer.twitter.com/en/docs/basics/rate-limits.html.

unique edge in the case of multiple retweets between the same two authors to favour diversity to quantity.

We present some statistics on *follow* and *retweet* graphs respectively in Tables 3 and 4. *Node count* includes the initial 50 root users, the rest being new users who interacted with root users. *Edge count* provides the number of unique interactions (we chose uniqueness for *retweet* and *follow* is unique by definition) between users. *Density* measures how much *potential graph space*, according to the number of nodes, interactions fill (*cf.* Eq. 2 with *Density*, the density for orientated graphs, *edgeCount*, the number of edges and *nodeCount*, the number of nodes). A first observation is the low density of both graphs that reflects a low interaction level in our sample.

$$Density = \frac{edgeCount}{nodeCount * (nodeCount - 1)/2} \qquad (2)$$

By definition, centrality measures do not give a direct answer to the question: *Who is an influencer*. Therefore, we preferred to rank users according to the scores rather than setting an empirical threshold which could skew the real answer to this question. To better get the contribution of centrality measures to influencer detection, we built a random user ranking as a baseline. As reference is based on a binary annotation instead of a ranking, we still need a specific metric to evaluate the final rankings. We thus selected Mean Average Precision (MAP) which was used for the same purpose in RepLab 2014. It is based on the IR principle which states that the most relevant results (here, the influencers) should appear in the highest positions of a ranking returned by a query system (here, requesting for influencers among some Twitter users). We compute MAP according to Eq. 2 with N, the total user count, n, the count of influencers correctly retrieved, $p(i)$, the precision at rank i (considering only the first i users), $R(i) = 1$ if the user at rank i is actually an influencer otherwise $R(i) = 0$.

$$MAP = \frac{1}{n} \sum_{i=1}^{N} p(i)R(i) \qquad (3)$$

Table 3. *Follow graph* statistics.

Number of nodes	5.067,480
Number of edges	5,149,491
Density	10^{-7}

Table 4. *Retweet graph* statistics.

Number of nodes	2099
Number of edges	2051
Density	10^{-4}

4.2 Results

Linguistic Approach

The results obtained indicate two ways of evaluating the pertinence of the linguistic features: (1) ROC-AUC curves comparing the system with and without the use of linguistic features and (2) ranking the features by order of importance to locate the position of linguistic features.

Figure 5 presents the ROC-AUC curves for both systems. We note that allowing a false positive rate of 30% the system with the linguistic features can reach a true positive rate of 82%.

Figure 6 presents the feature importance as extracted from the RF model. We note that the most important feature is the size of the post which naturally reflects the fact that linguistic phenomena such as argumentation or elongation are employed more often by users in longer messages. Interestingly, the use of premises (argumentation feature) as well as elongation (writing style feature) are shown to be important features.

We can thus see that the chart reveals that our selected linguistic features (argumentation and advising) find their place between two of the most often used non-linguistic features. This traces the path for the next steps in our research (Fig. 7).

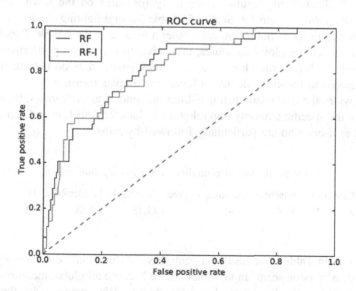

Fig. 6. ROC-AUC curve for both models.

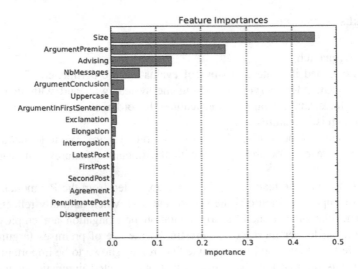

Fig. 7. Feature importance ordered by decreasing significance in the RF model.

Centrality Approach

We present in Table 5 the results of centrality measures on the *follow graph*. The statistics of the *follow graph* (*cf.* Sect. 4.1, Table 3), highlighting the low graph density, indicate that users do not follow each other a lot among the sample. PageRank and LeaderRank, which are global measures, take advantage from deep information about interactions through the graph but because of low density, they do not much improve results compared to Incoming degree, a local and simpler measure.

Hits provides the best result distinguishing influencers as *authorities*, thus showing relevance of the specific authority/hub relay for influencer detection and characterising influencers as users who are particularly followed by *hubs*.

Table 5. Results of centrality measures on *follow graph*.

Centrality	Baseline	Incoming degree	PageRank	LeaderRank	Hits
MAP (%)	38,67	43,49	44,25	44,53	51,68

We present in Table 6 the results of centrality measures on the *retweet graph*. The low graph density issue seems more difficult here because all global measures obtained the same results as the local one, *Incoming degree*. We explain it by the fact that information volume is lower for *retweet* thus it could make it even more difficult to be discriminative.

Hits does not get therefore the best result on the *retweet graph* as on the *follow graph*. This can be explained, as we previously indicated, by graph statistics rather than interaction types.

Table 6. Results of centrality measures on *retweet graph.*

Centrality	Baseline	Incoming degree	PageRank	LeaderRank	Hits
MAP (%)	38,67	40,91	40,91	40,91	40,91

5 Conclusion

In this paper, we have presented two studies that browse the two mains aspects of the influencers detection state-of-the-art and explore (1) the influence of linguistic features in forum conversations and (2) the importance of Twitter interaction types regarding centrality measures to find out particular user's positions reflecting their influence.

We designed a hybrid approach for the detection of influencers based on symbolic and statistical methods on the one hand and on the structure and textual content of the networks on the other hand. Our aim has been to address the significance of exploiting linguistic criteria (such as a user's argumentation, agreement/disagreement between users) for influence detection with respect to the traditionally used numerical criteria (number of responses, message size, number of relations, etc.). Our results confirm the relevance of the former in the detection of influence: the linguistic features pertaining to argumentation and writing style (in particular elongation) appear to be among the most relevant criteria.

We combined a selection of classical and complementary centrality measures on the one hand and Twitter interaction types we related to influence on the other hand. The goal has been to identify the combinations that help the most in identifying influential users in the interaction graphs we built. SNA shows a low interaction density issue while we selected root users from the same domain (bank). We shall increase the graph density to make the centrality measures more relevant. We could either try to «sum up» the graph by removing nodes with particularly low degree that do not give important information or build graphs from proper community detection.

The two independent studies allowed us to analyse two distinct types of approach that we intend to conjugate. Regarding both studies we have just presented, we consider various solutions to build a hybrid system based simultaneously on linguistic analysis and SNA.

A first solution would be to adapt the model learnt on forum to apply it on Twitter. We shall select linguistic features according to current results taking into consideration Twitter specificities. We shall evaluate it on tweets from the same user sample we used in this paper for comparability purposes. We shall also compute a hybrid influence score combining the aggregated score by user with (1) a centrality score obtained with the best structural modelling observed in this paper or (2) several centrality scores we shall weight according to their current respective result.

A second solution, more difficult to implement and that we shall also apply on the RepLab dataset, consists in enriching graph representation with linguistic information. For example, we shall represent the agreement between a user A and a user B by an edge from a node A to a node B. It is also possible to weight edges according to the importance we give to the information types they represent, including both raw and linguistic-based information. We shall finally apply centrality measures on the resulting multilayer graph.

The third and last solution is a combination at a larger scale as it includes a previous work on a dataset from the Change My View forum [23]. In this work, we have presented our approach to opinion change detection with the goal of identifying influencers by their effect, thus considering opinion change as an influencer's effect. We shall apply the linguistic model and centrality measures we have presented in this paper combining them with the opinion change detection module to detect influencers in the Change My View forum.

References

1. Richardson, M., Domingos, P.: Mining knowledge-sharing sites for viral marketing. In: Proceedings of the Eighth ACM SIGKDD International Conference on Knowledge Discovery and Data Mining, pp. 61–70. ACM (2002)
2. Bonacich, P.: Power and centrality: a family of measures. Am. J. Sociol. **92**(5), 1170–1182 (1987)
3. Page, L., Brin, S., Motwani R., Winograd, T.: The pagerank citation ranking: bringing order to the web. Technical report 1999-66 Stanford InfoLab, Stanford (1999)
4. Kien-Weng Tan, L., Na, J.C., Theng, Y.L.: Influence detection between blog posts through blog features, content analysis, and community identity. Online Inf. Rev. **35**(3), 425–442 (2011)
5. Rosenthal, S.: Detecting influencers in social media discussions. Ph.D. thesis, Columbia university, Columbia (2015)
6. Bavelas, A.: A mathematical model for group structures. Appl. Anthropol. **7**(3), 16–30 (1948)
7. Freeman, L.C.: Centrality in social networks conceptual clarification. Soc. Netw. **1**(3), 215–239 (1978)
8. Mariani, J., Paroubek, P., Francopoulo, G., Hamon, O.: Rediscovering 15 years of discoveries in language resources and evaluation: the LREC anthology analysis. In: Proceedings of LREC, pp. 26–31 (2014)
9. Sheikhahmadi, A., Nematbakhsh, M.A., Zareie, A.: Identification of influential users by neighbors in online social networks. Physica A **486**, 517–534 (2017)
10. Khadangi, E., Bagheri, A.: Presenting novel application-based centrality measures for finding important users based on their activities and social behavior. Comput. Hum. Behav. **73**, 64–79 (2017)
11. Dave, K., Bhatt, R., Varma, V.: Identifying influencers in social networks. In: Proceedings of the 5th International Conference on Weblogs and Social Media, pp. 1–9 (2011)
12. Ben Jabeur, L., Tamine, L., Boughanem, M.: Active microbloggers: identifying influencers, leaders and discussers in microblogging networks. In: Calderón-Benavides, L., González-Caro, C., Chávez, E., Ziviani, N. (eds.) SPIRE 2012. LNCS, vol. 7608, pp. 111–117. Springer, Heidelberg (2012). https://doi.org/10.1007/978-3-642-34109-0_12
13. Gionis, A., Terzi, E., Tsaparas, P.: Opinion maximization in social networks. In: Proceedings of 2013 SIAM International Conference on Data Mining, pp. 387–395 (2013)
14. Bigonha, C., Cardoso, T.N.C., Moro, M.M., Gonçalves, M.A., Almeida, V.A.: Sentiment-based influence detection on Twitter. J. Braz. Comput. Soc. **18**(3), 169–183 (2012)

15. Biran, O., Rosenthal, S., Andreas, J., McKeown, K., Rambow, O.: Detecting influencers in written online conversations. In: Proceedings of the Second Workshop on Language in Social Media, pp. 37–45. ACL (2012)
16. Quercia, D., Ellis, J., Capra, L., Crowcroft, J.: In the mood for being influential on Twitter. In: Proceedings of IEEE Third International Conference on Social Computing, pp. 307–314 (2011)
17. Hamzehei, A., Jiang, S., Koutra, D., Wong, R., Chen, F.: Topic-based social influence measurement for social networks. Australas. J. Inf. Syst. **21** (2017). http://journal.acs.org.au/index.php/ajis/article/view/1552
18. Weng, J., Lim, E.P., Jiang, J., He, Q.: Twitterrank: finding topic-sensitive influential twitterers. In: Proceedings of the Third ACM International Conference on Web Search and Data Mining, pp. 261–270. ACM (2010)
19. Katsimpras, G., Vogiatzis, D., Paliouras, G.: Determining influential users with supervised random walks. In: Proceedings of the 24th International Conference on World Wide Web, pp. 787–792. ACM, New York (2015)
20. Palau, R.M., Moens, M.F.: Argumentation mining: the detection, classification and structure of arguments in text. In: Proceedings of the 12th International Conference on Artificial Intelligence and Law (2009)
21. Amigó, E., et al.: Overview of RepLab 2014: author profiling and reputation dimensions for online reputation management. In: Kanoulas, E., et al. (eds.) CLEF 2014. LNCS, vol. 8685, pp. 307–322. Springer, Cham (2014). https://doi.org/10.1007/978-3-319-11382-1_24
22. Kleinberg, J.M.: Authoritative sources in a hyperlinked environment. J. ACM **46**(5), 604–632 (1999)
23. Lü, L., Zhang, Y.C., Yeung, C.H., Zhou, T.: Leaders in social networks, the delicious case. PLoS ONE **6**(6), e21202 (2011)
24. Deturck, K.: Détection d'influenceurs dans des médias sociaux. In: Proceedings of TALN 2018, vol. 2, pp. 117–130. ATALA (2018)

Video Intelligence as a Component of a Global Security System

Dominique Patrick Verdejo[1(✉)] and Eunika Mercier-Laurent[2]

[1] Personal Interactor, Montpellier and INHESJ, Paris, France
dominique.verdejo@personalinteractor.eu
[2] University Reims Champagne Ardenne, Reims, France
eunika.mercier-laurent@univ-reims.fr

Abstract. This paper describes the evolution of our research from video analytics to a global security system with focus on the video surveillance component. Indeed video surveillance has evolved from a commodity security tool up
to the most efficient way of tracking perpetrators when terrorism hits our modern
urban centers. As number of cameras soars, one could expect the system to
leverage the huge amount of data carried through the video streams to provide
fast access to video evidences, actionable intelligence for monitoring real-time
events and enabling predictive capacities to assist operators in their surveillance
tasks. This research explores a hybrid platform for video intelligence capture,
automated data extraction, supervised Machine Learning for intelligently
assisted urban video surveillance; Extension to other components of a global
security system are discussed.

Applying Knowledge Management principles in this research helps with deep
problem understanding and facilitates the implementation of efficient information and experience sharing decision support systems providing assistance to
people on the field as well as in operations centers. The originality of this work
is also the creation of "common" human-machine and machine to machine
language and a security ontology.

Keywords: Global security · Artificial Intelligence · Video · Surveillance ·
Ontology · Intelligence · Annotation · Natural language processing ·
Predictive analytics · Situational awareness · Big data ·
Knowledge Management · Eco-systems · Risk management · Machine learning

1 Introduction

Global digitalization has provided an extraordinary progress in communication and
services with their downside, the rise of threats in the ever growing cyber domain.
Increased terrorists' attacks and the rise of extremism require better management of all
available resources in aim to detect planned actions and prevent disasters [29]. The
complexity of security imposes considering all components and their interactions for
better understanding of causes. The third hype of Artificial Intelligence has introduced
powerful techniques for processing big data, used mainly in marketing at the beginning. Deep learning demonstrated great capacity in data processing; however the
complex challenges at stake require combining both data and knowledge processing in

© IFIP International Federation for Information Processing 2019
Published by Springer Nature Switzerland AG 2019
E. Mercier-Laurent and D. Boulanger (Eds.): AI4KM 2017, IFIP AICT 571, pp. 132–145, 2019.
https://doi.org/10.1007/978-3-030-29904-0_10

hybrid systems. Knowledge Management approach helps deep understanding of security problem and impacts, organizing and optimizing all sources, such as video records, exchanges in social networks, data collected from IoT, sensors and others in aim to set an adequate architecture of decision support system for all participants. Various AI techniques allows, among others, verifying consistency of gathered information and detect fake news for instance. AI also support the whole knowledge flow generated by all involved actors.

Global security deals with security of persons, of buildings, but also cybersecurity of IT systems by early detection of threats and weak signals in the cyberspace. This paper gives an overview of all components and focus on enhancing the human-machine effectiveness of surveillance activities, taking video surveillance as primary application field.

Besides traffic and cleanliness control, the role of cameras in urban areas and public transportation systems is mostly to deter crime, theft and vandalism. This is achieved through two distinct activities, one being real-time and the second, post-event. In real-time, the operators in urban control centers apply techniques to follow individuals of interest or to monitor specific areas or persons to protect from attacks. Those activities are often carried out in close collaboration with police staff.

Investigation of video records a posteriori consists in analyzing them to locate the meaningful footages that can be used as evidences in a court or intelligence to track perpetrators. These post-event video investigations are often long and fastidious, but prove more and more efficient to identify the perpetrators and lead to their arrest as image quality and resolution steadily improve. In both contexts, the tremendous increase of the number of cameras represents a major challenge for the overall efficiency of the system. It has been demonstrated that a human operator can monitor 16 cameras over a period of 20 min [3]. Whichever activity, real-time or post-event, requires attention of the operator on a number of video feeds. This highlights the need for computer based operator assistance.

This problem was already studied in our previous research - Vortex decision support system for video analysis [33]. The current research aims at improving the previous system by applying Knowledge Management principles and integrating a feedback from the previous work.

To predict possible threat scenarios, this research focuses, among others, on Machine Learning models to process specific pattern matching in spatiotemporal event sequences. However the prediction based on past data is insufficient to predict the future disasters. The permanent metamorphosis of threats prevents from constructing a sufficiently representative and properly documented data set for system training. Surveillance activities using video, social media and cyber defense data have one common point: they all capture and manipulate highly varied, complex and unpredictable events and behaviors, for which risk assessment requires mostly human common sense and contextual knowledge. Connection with the other sources of information and knowledge, such as the law enforcement files in the case of terrorism is necessary for overall understanding.

While related research focuses on media analysis, like video analysis, providing added forensic evidence research capabilities, we have chosen to emphasize on the analysis of metadata generated by such algorithms. These metadata can be efficiently used to establish correlations with other media analysis results like social networks or events generated by cyber security monitoring systems.

The applied bottom-up Knowledge Management approach combined with knowledge modelling allows easy extension to the others system components of global security, i.e. social networks analysis and cybersecurity, especially in the era of ubiquitous IoT and drones equipped with facial recognition capabilities.

After the general introduction and pointing out the challenge, this paper describes our research method, followed by the state of the art in the fields covered. The explanation on the role of Knowledge Management in this research is provided before we focus on the first system component of this research-hybrid decision support system for real-time video analysis. Conclusions and some perspectives of future work and applications are given at the end.

2 Research Method

Considering our experience acquired during the initial work on Vortex project we decided to consider the video analysis as a part of a Global Security system. Currently, the proposed research method applies Knowledge Management and complex problem solving [34] to global security. It consists in understanding the challenge of a global security system and aims at (i) proposing a modular architecture for a hybrid system, (ii) prototype and test separate modules conceived by combining holistic and system approaches. Each component plays its own role and interacts with the others for more accurate result. Incremental approach allows building the whole system step by step. At each stage, the adequate AI techniques are selected and tested and results discussed.

The role of Knowledge Management consists in

- Problem analysis with a given context. What data/information/knowledge do we need to successfully manage security and prevent disasters provoked by ill-intentioned people? What sources of data/information/knowledge are available?
- Initiating and managing a human-machine self-reinforcing synergy
- Defining the overall architecture of the decision support (not making) system, considering all involved actors' contributions and needs.
- Building generic and reusable knowledge models (static, dynamic or hybrid, ex. multi-agents systems).
- Defining a strategy for future extensions (Building blocs)
- Integrating a feedback on all stages.

Related to video analysis, we propose to transpose the general scene analysis problem into a natural language description exercise. This approach allows human operators to share understanding of the scene/situation with the machine. This common language, scene description capability, creates a gate between human and machine providing two major benefits: (i) situational awareness knowledge can be immediately shared between operators without visual support and (ii) the human operators can enrich the description provided by the machine with additional common sense or contextual knowledge.

This natural language processing approach will use ontologies as a model for text generation and a semantic navigation tool. This provides guidelines to keep consistency, manage ambiguities and act as a communication protocol dedicated to a specific media analysis.

The machine learns text generation through supervised machine learning (labeling) approach and builds risk scenarios using reinforced learning. The scenarios of maximum risk likelihood will be proposed to the operators for facing the most urgent challenge in modern control centers: monitoring exponentially growing numbers of sensors inputs.

This module will be considered using modularity, genericity and reusability approach for future extensions.

3   State of the Art

Research in video analysis is not new. French programs PRIAM and RIAM initiated by the French Ministry of Industry gave some promising results in applying AI techniques for video analysis on the flow. For example, the architecture of MediaWorks combined neural networks, multi-agent systems and natural language processing for relevant finding on the flow of person or object to illustrate TV news [4]. These projects did not address security issues as the subject was not as critical at this time.

Since 2000, many researches have been made in semantic video indexing [4] and European Research has been funded to create tools to annotate and retrieve video [5]. It is commonly agreed today that we need an abstract layer of representation, a language, to describe and retrieve video. Ontologies have been proposed as an adapted tool to capture observations but also to shift domains as surveillance can be operated on media from many different natures depending on the activity [6–8] (satellite, urban, cyber, social networks, etc.).

The "Smart City" trend combining technological progress, cameras price drop down and raise of delinquency, has prompted cities to install surveillance systems. However they did not have a resource for systematic analysis of the recorded content. The raise of terrorist's attacks amplified a demand for efficient video surveillance systems.

The effectiveness of such systems depends on intelligence in exploring the available data sources of information and knowledge.

The analysis after the disaster pointed out the need for preventive actions.

Opening of public data and Big Data from multiple sources are available but using only analytics on the past data is insufficient for prevention of future disasters. We did not find in available literature the efficient decision support system to face this challenge. Some separate modules, such as video analytics, social networks mining, OSINT (Open Source Intelligence) and IoT data exploring are only described.

3.1   Evolution of Video Surveillance

Learning from human generated annotations, the machine has shown a capacity to generalize, identifying objects and generating text sentences describing image and scenes. In 2017, this effort is extended to video with the DAVIS [14] challenge on video object segmentation. The downside of this approach, is that human contribution is highly necessary to generate meaningful datasets. Initiatives to deploy crowd-annotations platform have been recently undertaken to improve and speed-up the ground truth collection from users on the Web [13], fostering the need for creation of machine learning datasets.

It is notable that image segmentation, object recognition, video labeling creates a leap frog in surveillance applications and human interface. But, as every camera turns into a talkative witness, we lack the ability to correlate the different sources and enable global risk analysis. This is particularly important for behaviour analysis and anomaly detection in scene understanding, including gesture and intentions analysis.

3.2   Evolution and Revolution of Video Analytics

Over the past 15 years, numerous tests and benchmarks were undertaken to assess feasibility of using algorithms to perform recognition of specific situations to ease the task of video operators. It is expected that automating video monitoring can lead to a less heavy mental workload for operators as their attention can be focused only on identified problems. In fact, false alarms tend to overcrowd the video monitoring environment and have rendered those technologies quite useless in most operational cases, specifically in large urban surveillance contexts.

Traditional video analytics, based on bitmap analysis can be useful to identify line crossing or counter-flow. They can count individuals and detect crowds and abandoned luggage. But they fail providing insights on more complex situations like fights, tagging, thefts and carjacking where more context and common sense is required [10]. Highly focused European FP7 2010–2013 research project, VANAHEIM] [9] has been developed in the context of two metro stations and revealed the difficulty to use inputs from video analytics modules to automate the displays on video walls. Nevertheless this project has been pivotal in demonstrating the huge potential of unsupervised video analysis and the detection of abnormality into long recordings.

Since 2010, a revolution has begun in video analytics. Thanks to Convolutional Neural Networks, Deep Learning techniques, object recognition, image segmentation and labeling has shown impressively efficient, up to the point where the machine, using a software built on top of GoogLeNet has demonstrated in 2015 an ability to identify objects in still images that is almost identical to humans [12]. This was made possible thanks to the availability of a very large image dataset called Imagenet [10] (over 1,4 million images from over 1000 classes) manually annotated and a challenge that took place annually between 2010 and 2015, the ImageNet Large Scale Visual Recognition Challenge (ILSVRC). In 2015, the Chinese company BAIDU also claimed actual superiority of machine image recognition compared to human on the same image dataset [11].

3.3   Evolution of Cyber Security and Cyber Defense

Information systems security has evolved since 2000 taking into account the global interconnection of machines. System protection has evolved from basic anti-virus and firewalls up to a range of monitoring activities dedicated to detect and identify intrusions and potentially harmful activities on the networks and servers. Recently, companies have marketed AI based systems to achieve specific surveillance analysis, based on the logs produced by applications and systems. Interestingly, those new approaches, gathered around the SIEM components (Security Incident Event Management) tend to procure a behavioral analysis rather than a simple event categorization.

It is worth mentioning the similarities between video and cyber analytics which both converge toward behavioral analysis for detecting the weak signals in the massive data sets.

Cyber Security for instance, uses dedicated event description and exchange named STIX [31] to communicate cyber threat intelligence.

3.4   Evolution of Social Network Analysis

In complex situations such as terrorism and cybercrime analysis of video is not sufficient. Social networks and especially ephemeral ones are used to spread information and to recruit new terrorists by systematic brainwashing. [14] describes detection of influential users using linguistic approach. [15] uses graphs and networks (Social Networks Analysis-SNA) to detect leaders in the "dark networks".

Social Network Analysis is now widely used [23] as a fully operational intelligence source, introducing the SOCMINT [26] neologism standing for Social Media Intelligence.

3.5   Knowledge Management for Global Security

Security management requires deep understanding of a given problem in its context and follows the rules of KM lifecycle: acquisition, modeling, navigation and use. The adequate AI techniques will support the whole process [25].

Global Security is composed of a set of domains security systems, each having its own objectives and controls. As threat awareness requires surveillance, each domain uses specific surveillance processes and vocabulary.

Knowledge Management helps organizing and optimizing the available sources of data/information and knowledge and creating progressively a common language for all involved actors to facilitate exchanges between them [32]. Three main approaches can be used: top-down, bottom-up and combination of both. In the case of global security a well-defined and dynamic strategy is mandatory to efficiently face the threats. Dynamic strategy allows flexibility for quick adaptation to evolving situation. Conceptual knowledge modelling as for ex ontologies allow reusing knowledge for related applications.

The existing literature provides description of all facets of security, useful for building such a system [24]. In this work, Rogers analyses the legacy of the Cold War's proliferation of weapons of mass destruction; the impact of human activity on the global ecosystem; the growth of hyper capitalism and resulting poverty and insecurity; the competition for energy resources and strategic minerals; biological warfare. This context leads to delinquency. Similar conclusion was stated at the end of colloquium organized by French Ministry of Defense on the influence of Climate change on the rise of crime [34].

Chen [26] describes Terrorism informatics as methodologies and integrate process of gathering and processing all related information.

We also found works applying KM principles to water and food security and to multiple risks management.

In our case Knowledge Management applied to global security system will connect components shown in Fig. 1.

On our knowledge, there is no integrated approach of Knowledge Management to global security; this and the need for a systemic approach is leitmotiv for our research.

Our proposal is then to consider the feedback from previous approach in the light of such global security system.

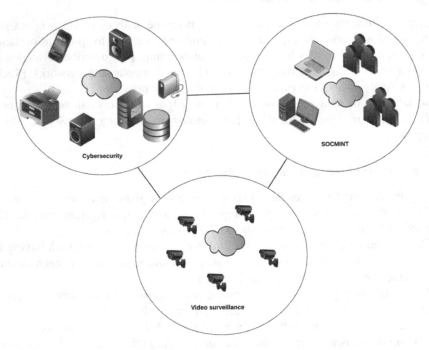

Fig. 1. Main interrelated components of global security system

4   Feedback Form the Previous Research

The research on video analysis, under the name of VORTEX project, has been initiated in 2010 in France after a large number of interviews with system architects, security managers and police officers. The aim was to spot the flaws of contemporary metropolitan video surveillance systems and propose an optimization of human activities in video surveillance operations. A synthetic article about public-private partnerships in new video surveillance services, for the French National Institute of Security and Justice (INHESJ), was written subsequently.

Findings described in this initial stage of the research where the following: As video surveillance moves through its digital transformation from analog cables, monitors and tapes to a complete computer based environment, there is a quantum leap in both numbers of video sensors and geographic scale of systems deployed. Large French urban areas like Paris, Lyon, Marseille and Nice have set up or are in the process of setting up systems with more than one thousand cameras, without mentioning the thousands of cameras already scattered along the public transportation lines and inside the vehicles [1]. While the need for police activity monitoring surges, these numbers are also increased by the new body worn cameras on police officers. Information Technology provides solutions to record and visualize all these cameras, but it does not meet the day to day exploitation needs made more complex by the multitude of video sensors. In a word, the capacity to have an eye everywhere does not spare the people watching. A global rethinking of the balance between people in front line, people in operations centers as well as citizens must be undertaken. We introduce the need for a rethinking and rationalization of the human role in image interpretation, based on the finding that we can deploy much more than we can actually monitor. It is made necessary to define how a human operator can collect and preserve intelligence [2] from video sources, with the aid of the machine, assuming the large number of video feeds creates a rich potential information source. This in turns requires new training procedures and new tools to be created to cope with system scale and carry out this strategic task.

Subsequent research emphasized the importance of a contextual use of video, in complement of other data sources.

Wise decision making require considering all available sources on a given topic as well as the knowledge about the current context. Recent attacks, notably on energy critical infrastructures [28] show that infrastructure security may be endangered by cyber-attacks. This is leading to the creation of a hybrid domain for security called Cyber Physical Security (CPS) [27, 30] with social networks as platforms of choice for preparing operational details in such cases.

In this context, Vortex project objectives are to keep the human operator at the heart of the system and decision process. This requires the development of computer aided monitoring automation, providing advices and recommendations as to what should be watched first in the continuous flow of contextual real-time and recorded events.

5 Research Focus – Hybrid System for Video Analysis

Those breakthroughs in image and video analysis and labeling are the cornerstones of VORTEX concept. But as we witness the need for developing supervised machine learning processes that can lead to development of video intelligence expert modules, we also realize that in the ever changing very complex metropolitan environment, the patterns of normality and abnormality and their relationship to the images captured by the cameras are difficult to express. The role of the human operator in the heart of the semantic system is mandatory to reconcile volumes of data captured by computerized video sensors with contextual situation awareness. Reinforcement learning [30] is a machine learning technique sitting at the crossing of supervised and unsupervised learning. It implies defining a decision function that allows the machine to modify its state and also to define rewards and penalty functions that are used to provide the machine with an assessment of the result of its decisions. Using a very large number of try and fail the machine infers an optimized solution by maximizing its reward.

We therefore propose an approach based on two distinct annotation processes. One being conducted through the most modern labeling algorithms running on state of the art, dedicated hardware platforms, or inference platforms, the second being performed by the operators. We introduce a third knowledge based situational awareness module or recommendation module that uses insights produced from the analysis of combined human and machine generated annotations and communicates back its recommendations to the operator. This system is able of maintaining long term memory of what is a "normal" or "abnormal" situation and in addition has the essential capability to take into account human generated alerts and comments to adapt to new situations as they happen.

Replaced in the context of video surveillance, the human operator appears even more important to machine learning as he not only recognizes objects and people but assesses the level of risk of a particular situation and correlates scenes monitored by different cameras.

From the picture in Fig. 2. it is made clear that the System is fed with annotations coming primarily from human operators' interactions witnessing events happening on their surveillance screens (traffic incidents, aggressions and thefts, vandalism, tags, terrorist attacks, smuggling…). This human input is key to providing a common sense context to information that is provided automatically by labeling modules either embedded directly in the cameras or located centrally in the cloud System.

The supervised learning is then operated by human rating of situations on a severity scale, enabling the System to learn and anticipate situations contexts leading to potential risky situations.

The RETEX[1] describes that anticipation data which is deduced by the system while streams of new data flows continuously from both operators and cameras. These streams can also be completed by auxiliary data streams incoming from contextual communication systems and metadata concerning the sensors. The RETEX provides a predictive capacity based on the supervised learning achieved continuously by the interaction of operators and System. An important part of the System analytics is dedicated to transform the RETEX, primarily made of textual content, into actual operational data that can be actioned by operators. In the context of video surveillance, this is achieved by highlighting those cameras that are most important to watch.

5.1   Situational Awareness Increased with Video Surveillance

The RETEX illustrates how the predictive capabilities of the System can be turned into prescriptive surveillance actions. Still, state of the art video surveillance management system provide poor interfaces to enable operators to capture their annotations on the fly and store them in a workable format.

---

[1] RETEX is "Retour d'Experience" in French in the text (feedback from experience).

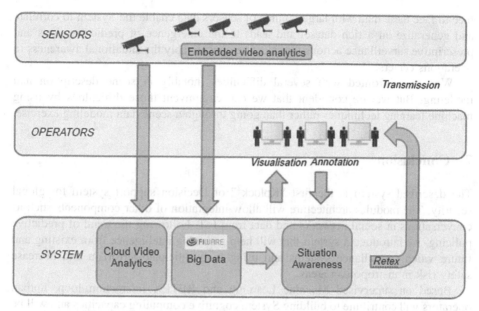

Fig. 2. Human centric design for man-machine interoperability

It is thus one of the key objectives of this research to study the conditions of an efficient real-time annotation to enable the operators to achieve the necessary supervised learning and initialize the RETEX loop. Information captured by operators are essential to a sound indexing of video and participate to the overall indexing required by both forensic investigations and day to day exploitation.

6   Originality of This Work

VORTEX is proposing a genuine approach to the man machine cooperation by leveraging the recent breakthroughs in Machine Learning technologies that allows processing video from traditional stationary cameras as well as mobile or handheld devices [16]. Based on the essential finding that the video media needs to be translated to be workable, we propose to organize a data model for streaming information generated by video analytics labeling algorithms. We propose to define the annotation interfaces necessary to capture operators' annotation in real-time in such a way as it can be used as input for a supervised learning input. Eventually, we propose a predictive analytics System capable of issuing recommendations to the human operators and interacting with them in a feedback loop (RETEX) of reinforcement learning.

It is important to note that annotations as well as any other indexing data may be stored and preserved much beyond the limits of video retention periods, as advised for instance by the European Data Protection Supervisor (EDPS). This means that real-time automated labeling data are key to provide large datasets of surveillance contexts without the burden of keeping the video they originated from. VORTEX is an attempt to rationalize the capture of human feedback in surveillance and crisis context. Putting face to face these data with large volume of sensors data enable the System to correlate and generalize on a rich dataset and leads to the emergence of predictive alerts and prescriptive surveillance actions that increase considerably the situational awareness in operations centers.

We are confronted with several difficulties, notably in scene description and modeling. But we are confident that we can circumvent those difficulties by using machine learning techniques rather than going through a scene data modeling exercise.

7   Conclusion

The described system is the first "Kblock[2]" of Decision support system for global security. The modular architecture will allow integration of other components such as conversations in social networks and data from IoT. Following the trend of predictive policing, we introduce a system that will help gathering intelligence from existing and future video surveillance systems and using it to anticipate terrorism and decrease safety risk in metropolitan areas.

Based on supervised Machine Learning and RETEX interaction loop, human operators will contribute to building System cognitive computing capacities and will be augmented in return by its prescriptive analytics.

Universality of this approach consists in the following: it does not depend on video surveillance technology infrastructure but complements it with new video analytics labeling systems, new annotation and communication tools and new predictive capabilities.

The security ontology [20] definition is the basis of the underlying knowledge management required to provide a consistent framework that will serve as an inter-operability guide to extend the approach to different countries and open intelligence cooperation between agencies, both nationally and internationally, representing a potential benefit for global organizations like EUROPOL. Moreover, the genericity of the model for risk management can be extended from video surveillance to cyberse-curity to SOCMINT and to all surveillance activities.

Adopting an ontology and developing automated labeling capacities provides the ground for generating a continuous stream of data flowing from the many and highly diversified sources of information available, both video sensors and human inputs. Among human inputs we can cite metropolitan security control centers operators, but also social networks OSINT (Open Source Intelligence) or even SOCMINT (Social Media Intelligence) which play an ever increasing role in situational awareness. A mixt fusion approach based on cognitive computing, could then benefit large scale proven systems like IBM Watson [17] to extract early signals and anticipate risks from the very large textual information generated in such context.

---

[2] Knowledge block.

8 Perspective and Future Work

VORTEX framework has been conceived for aiding urban video surveillance operations, but similar initiatives have been undertaken in the field of aerial image analytics [18] and the knowledge based information fusion proposed for the System has been under scrutiny in numerous other papers [19]. The range of sensors providing field data is not limited to stationary cameras. Ground vehicle cameras, aerial drone cameras, body-worn cameras, microphones and general presence detection sensors output information streams that can be injected in the RETEX interaction loop.

The real-time annotation tool may be utilized by operators supervising media different from urban surveillance cameras, i.e. thermal cameras, radars, LIDARs as well as front-line operators located directly in the zone of interest and providing direct field intelligence to the System.

Different application field also requiring human surveillance, like cyber security, may be using VORTEX framework by adapting the vocabulary of annotations. This is made possible by using domain dependent Ontologies, as mentioned in previous projects.

Acknowledgements. Inception of this research was presented in 2012 to the Aerospace competitiveness cluster PEGASE [21], now part of the larger "Pôle Risques" [22] in France where it got a distinction for its "usefulness in the aerial vehicles data processing allowing drones and stratospheric machines to achieve their mission".

Academic Partnerships. VORTEX concept was elaborated in cooperation with two laboratories, the LIRMM from Montpellier University, expert in machine learning and the LUTIN from Paris VIII, specialized in man machine interfaces, detection and semantics of human perceived actions.

References

1. CODREANU, Dana, Thèse de doctorat IRIT, UMR 55, Université Paul Sabatier, sous la direction de Florence SEDES, "Modélisation des métadonnées spatio-temporelles associées aux contenus vidéos et interrogation de ces métadonnées à partir des trajectoires hybrides: Application dans le contexte de la vidéosurveillance (2015)
2. [Bremond 08] Francois BREMOND, «Interprétation de scène et video-surveillance», AViRS 2008 (Analyse Video pour le Renseignement et la Sécurité, Paris (2008)
3. Malochet, V., Jagu, T.: Surveiller à distance. Une ethnographie des opérateurs municipaux de vidéosurveillance, p. 62. IAU-IDF (2011)
4. Golbreich, C.: Vers un moteur de recherche évolué de documents multimédia par le contenu. Rapport interne, Université Rennes, 2 (2000)
5. Vezzani, R., Cucchiara, R.: ViSOR: video surveillance on-line repository for annotation retrieval. In: 2008 IEEE International Conference on Multimedia and Expo, pp. 1281–1284. IEEE (2008)
6. Francois, A.R., Nevatia, R., Hobbs, J., Bolles, R.C., Smith, J.R.: VERL: an ontology framework for representing and annotating video events. IEEE Multimedia 12(4), 76–86 (2005)

7. Luther, M., Mrohs, B., Wagner, M., Steglich, S., Kellerer, W.: Situational reasoning-a practical OWL use case. In: Proceedings of Autonomous Decentralized Systems, ISADS 2005, pp. 461–468. IEEE, April 2005

8. Hernandez-Leal, P., Escalante, H.J., Sucar, L.E.: Towards a generic ontology for video surveillance. In: Sucar, E., Mayora, O., Muñoz de Cote, E. (eds.) Applications for Future Internet. LNICST, vol. 179, pp. 3–7. Springer, Cham (2017). https://doi.org/10.1007/978-3-319-49622-1_1

9. Odobez, J.-M., et al.: Unsupervised Activity Analysis and Monitoring Algorithms for Effective Surveillance Systems. In: Fusiello, A., Murino, V., Cucchiara, R. (eds.) ECCV 2012. LNCS, vol. 7585, pp. 675–678. Springer, Heidelberg (2012). https://doi.org/10.1007/978-3-642-33885-4_80

10. Russakovsky, O., et al.: (* = equal contribution) ImageNet large scale visual recognition challenge. In: IJCV (2015)

11. Wu, R., Yan, S., Shan, Y., Dang, Q., Sun, G.: Deep image: scaling up image recognition. arXiv preprint arXiv:1501.02876 **7**(8) (2015)

12. http://davischallenge.org/index.html. Accessed 2018

13. Kavasidis, I., Palazzo, S., Di Salvo, R., Giordano, D., Spampinato, C.: An innovative web-based collaborative platform for video annotation. Multimedia Tools Appl. **70**(1), 413–432 (2014)

14. Patel, N., Lopez, C., Partalas, I., Avouac, P.A., Segond, F.: Detecting Influential Users in Social Network Conversations: A Linguistic Approach (2017)

15. Berzinji, A.: Detecting Key Players in Terrorist Networks (2011). http://uu.diva-portal.org/smash/get/diva2:442516/FULLTEXT01.pdf

16. Ferrari, S., et al.: Convolutional-Features Analysis and Control for Mobile Visual Scene Perception (2017)

17. IBM Watson: How Cognitive Computing Can Be Applied to Big Data Challenges in Life Sciences Research - Clinical Therapeutics - 2016/04/01/Chen, Ying, Elenee Argentinis Weber, Griff. http://www.sciencedirect.com/science/article/pii/S0149291815013168

18. Solbrig, P., Bulatov, D., Meidow, J., Wernerus, P., Thonnessen, U.: Online annotation of airborne surveillance and reconnaissance videos. In: 2008 11th International Conference on Information Fusion, pp. 1–8. IEEE June 2008

19. Smart, P.R., Shadbolt, N.R., Carr, L.A., Schraefel, M.C.: Knowledge-based information fusion for improved situational awareness. In: 2005 8th International Conference on Information Fusion, vol. 2, pp. 8-pp. IEEE, July 2005

20. Luther, M., Mrohs, B., Wagner, M., Steglich, S., Kellerer, W.: Situational reasoning-a practical OWL use case. In: Proceedings of the Autonomous Decentralized Systems, ISADS 2005, pp. 461–468. IEEE, April 2005

21. http://competitivite.gouv.fr/identify-a-cluster/a-cluster-s-datasheet-910/pegase-59/pegase-62/pegase-63.html?cHash=8fd7e29039de6042eb42f8768d51f8df

22. http://www.safecluster.com/

23. Andrews, S., Brewster, B., Day, T.: Organised crime and social media: a system for detecting, corroborating and visualising weak signals of organised crime online. Secur. Inf. **7**(1), 3 (2018)

24. Rogers, P.: Losing Control: Global Security in the Twenty-first Century, 3rd edn, 256 p. Pluto Press (2010). ISBN-13: 978-0745329376

25. Strous, L.: Should artificial intelligence be more regulated? In: Strous, L., Cerf, Vinton G. (eds.) IFIPIoT 2018. IAICT, vol. 548, pp. 28–34. Springer, Cham (2019). https://doi.org/10.1007/978-3-030-15651-0_4

26. Chen, H., Reid, E., Sinai, J., Silke, A., Ganor, B.: Terrorism Informatics: Knowledge Management and Data Mining for Homeland Security. Springer, New York (2008). https://doi.org/10.1007/978-0-387-71613-8
27. Katina, P.F., Keating, C.B.: Cyber-physical systems governance: a framework for (meta) cybersecurity design. In: Masys, A.J. (ed.) Security by Design. ASTSA, pp. 137–169. Springer, Cham (2018). https://doi.org/10.1007/978-3-319-78021-4_7
28. Venkatachary, S.K., Prasad, J., Samikannu, R.: Cybersecurity and cyber terrorism-in energy sector–a review. J. Cyber Secur. Technol. 2(3–4), 111–130 (2018)
29. Narayanan, S., Ganesan, A., Joshi, K., Oates, T., Joshi, A., Finin, T.: Cognitive Techniques for Early Detection of Cybersecurity Events. arXiv preprint arXiv:1808.00116 (2018)
30. Li, C., Qiu, M.: Reinforcement Learning for Cyber-Physical Systems: with Cybersecurity Case Studies. CRC Press (2019)
31. Sadique, F., Cheung, S., Vakilinia, I., Badsha, S., Sengupta, S.: Automated structured threat information expression (STIX) document generation with privacy preservation. In: 2018 9th IEEE Annual Ubiquitous Computing, Electronics & Mobile Communication Conference (UEMCON) (IEEE UEMCON 2018) (2018)
32. Mercier-Laurent, E.: Innovation Ecosystems. Wiley (2011)
33. Verdejo, D.: Supervised Machine Learning Video Intelligence Platform and Knowledge Management for improved Situational Awareness 14 July 2017 publication description AI4KM/IJCAI 2017 (2017)
34. Defense et climat - quels enjeux? - La Revue stratégique de défense et de sécurité nationale, octobre 2017. https://www.defense.gouv.fr/dgris/recherche-et-prospective/prospective-de-defense/defense-et-climat

Author Index

Printed in the United States
By Bookmasters